LANGENSCHEIDT-LEKTÜRE 60

HUMOROUS SHORT STORIES

ENGLISCH

4	**Strange Adventures**	Abenteuergeschichten, die sich besonderer Beliebtheit erfreuen.
13	**13 Whodunits**	Kriminalgeschichten u.a. von Agatha Christie, O. Henry und Saki.
15	**Laugh and Be Merry!**	Köstlicher britischer Humor in Short Stories und Witzen.
42	**Short Stories**	Ausgesuchte Erzählungen, die sich durch ihren hervorragenden Stil auszeichnen.
60	**Humorous Short Stories**	Spaßige Situationskomik und amüsante Schlaglichter auf englische Originalität.
61	**The Birds/Kiss Me Again, Stranger**	Hier – die Vorlage für Hitchcocks Thriller, dazu ein weiterer Shocker.
66	**A Steinbeck Reader**	Vier Kurzgeschichten des großen amerikanischen Erzählers.
67	**Murder! Murder? Murder!**	Fünf Mordgeschichten und fünf ungewöhnliche Täter – besonders spannende Lektüren.
70	**So spricht der Amerikaner!**	Eine kleine Einführung in das Amerikanische Englisch.
71	**Spotlights**	15 englische und amerikanische Kurzgeschichten.
72	**Scoundrels**	Zwei leichte englische Kurzgeschichten.

FRANZÖSISCH

44	**Nouvelles françaises**	Eine Sammlung literarisch interessanter französischer Novellen.
57	**Textes français modernes**	Humoristische und ernste „Auskünfte" über historische und kulturgeschichtliche Themen.
59	**Images de la France**	Französische Texte über Land und Leute.
62	**Thanatos Palace Hotel**	Novellistische Kostbarkeiten, wie sie nur aus der Feder André Maurois' fließen können.
68	**Humour à gogo**	Typische Witze sind in diesem Lektüreband mit humorvollen Kurzgeschichten vereinigt.

ITALIENISCH

7	**Un po' di tutto**	Aktuelle Einblicke in die Verhältnisse des Landes und in das Geistesleben des Volkes.
69	**Storie poliziesche**	Moderne italienische Kriminalgeschichten – sie halten den Leser bis zur letzten Seite gefangen.

RUSSISCH

55	**Moderne russische Erzählungen**	Typische Kurzgeschichten, teils humoristisch, teils ernst.
56	**Leichte russische Kurzgeschichten**	Populäre Aufsätze, Anekdoten, Sprichwörter und Kurzgeschichten.

SPANISCH

36	**Cuentos españoles**	Charakteristische Erzählungen aus dem spanischen Volksleben.
58	**Lecturas amenas**	Humorvolle Erzählungen in spanischer Umgangssprache.
65	**Rodando por España**	Interessante Einblicke in das Alltagsleben des spanischen Volkes.

Langenscheidt-Lektüre 60

Humorous Short Stories

5 humorvolle englische Kurzgeschichten

von P. G. Wodehouse, Frank O'Connor und Herbert Sutherland

LANGENSCHEIDT

BERLIN · MÜNCHEN · LEIPZIG · WIEN · ZÜRICH · NEW YORK

Die inhaltliche Auswahl und Bearbeitung dieses Bandes erfolgte durch Dr. Margarete Haag

Auflage: 15. 14. 13. 12. | Letzte Zahlen
Jahr: 1997 | maßgeblich

Druck: Druckhaus Langenscheidt, Berlin-Schöneberg
Printed in Germany · ISBN 3-468-44600-4

Vorwort

Es gibt einen spezifisch englischen Humor. Das ist unbestritten, aber sobald man versucht, ihn zu definieren, begibt man sich auf schwankenden Boden: Nonsense und Wortspiele und . . .? Die fünf Kurzgeschichten dieses Bandes sagen mehr über den englischen Humor aus, als es Definitionen vermögen. Wer sind die Autoren?
P. G. Wodehouse ist unter den Humoristen sicherlich "the greatest living writer of English" (*The Times 12. 10. 71*). Seine literarische Produktion umfaßt 90 Bücher mit vielgelesenen Romanen und Kurzgeschichten. Gleich dem alten Schelmenroman reiht er eine humorvolle Episode an die andere. Seine köstliche Situationskomik und seine schrulligen englischen Originale machen ihn zu einem Meister des englischen Humors.
Die Komik der Erzählungen von Frank O'Connor und Herbert Sutherland ist gleichfalls umwerfend; sie zeigt jedoch andere Facetten des englischen Humors. In O'Connors Geschichten ist die humoristische Komponente stiller und feiner - aber deswegen keineswegs weniger vergnüglich und liebenswert.

Dieser Band bringt für die Übersetzungshilfen eine Besonderheit. Wörter, die in der Vokabelspalte enthalten sind, werden im laufenden Text mit einem kleinen Kreis gekennzeichnet. Der Leser erspart sich dadurch vergebliches Suchen. Er kommt schneller voran.

LANGENSCHEIDT

Inhaltsverzeichnis

Erklärung der Aussprachebezeichnung

A. Vokale und Diphthonge

[ɑː] reines langes a, wie in Vater, kam, Schwan: *far* [fɑː], *father* [ˈfɑːðə].

[ʌ] kommt im Deutschen nicht vor. Kurzes dunkles a, bei dem die Lippen nicht gerundet sind. Vorn und offen gebildet: *butter* [ˈbʌtə], *come* [kʌm], *colour* [ˈkʌlə], *blood* [blʌd], *flourish* [ˈflʌriʃ], *twopence* [ˈtʌpəns].

[æ] heller, ziemlich offener, nicht zu kurzer Laut. Raum zwischen Zunge und Gaumen noch größer als bei ä in Ähre: *fat* [fæt], *man* [mæn].

[ɛə] nicht zu offenes halblanges ä; im Englischen nur vor r, das als ein dem ä nachhallendes ə erscheint: *bare* [bɛə], *pair* [pɛə], *there* [ðɛə].

[ai] Bestandteile: helles, zwischen ɑː und æ liegendes a und schwächeres offenes i. Die Zunge hebt sich halbwegs zur i-Stellung: *I* [ai], *lie* [lai], *dry* [drai].

[au] Bestandteile: helles, zwischen ɑː und æ liegendes a und schwächeres offenes u: *house* [haus], *now* [nau].

[ei] halboffenes e, nach i auslautend, indem die Zunge sich halbwegs zur i-Stellung hebt: *date* [deit], *play* [plei], *obey* [əˈbei].

[e] halboffenes kurzes e, etwas geschlossener als das e in Bett: *bed* [bed], *less* [les].

[ə] flüchtiger Gleitlaut, ähnlich dem deutschen, flüchtig gesprochenen e in Gelage: *about* [əˈbaut], *butter* [ˈbʌtə], *connect* [kəˈnekt].

[əu] mit [ə] beginnend und in schwaches u auslautend; keine Rundung der Lippen, kein Heben der Zunge: *note* [nəut], *boat* [bəut], *below* [biˈləu].

[iː] langes i, wie in lieb, Bibel, aber etwas offener einsetzend als im Deutschen; wird in Südengland doppellautig gesprochen, indem sich die Zunge allmählich zur i-Stellung hebt: *scene* [siːn], *sea* [siː], *feet* [fiːt], *ceiling* [ˈsiːliŋ].

[i] kurzes offenes i wie in bin, mit: *big* [big], *city* [ˈsiti].

[iə] halboffenes halblanges i mit nachhallendem ə: *here* [hiə], *hear* [hiə], *inferior* [inˈfiəriə].

[ɔː] offener langer, zwischen a und o schwebender Laut: *fall* [fɔːl], *nought* [nɔːt], *or* [ɔː], *before* [biˈfɔː].

[ɔ] offener kurzer, zwischen a und o schwebender Laut, offener als das o in Motte: *god* [gɔd], *not* [nɔt], *wash* [wɔʃ], *hobby* [ˈhɔbi].

[ɔi] Bestandteile: offenes o und schwächeres offenes i. Die Zunge hebt sich halbwegs zur i-Stellung: *voice* [vɔis], *boy* [bɔi], *annoy* [əˈnɔi].

[əː] im Deutschen fehlender Laut; offenes langes ö, etwa wie gedehnt gesprochenes ö in öffnen, Mörder; kein Vorstülpen oder Runden der Lippen; kein Heben der Zunge: *word* [wəːd], *girl* [gəːl], *learn* [ləːn], *murmur* [ˈməːmə].

[uː] langes u wie in Buch, doch ohne Lippenrundung; vielfach diphthongisch als halboffenes langes u mit nachhallendem geschlossenem u: *fool* [fuːl], *shoe* [ʃuː], *you* [juː], *rule* [ruːl], *canoe* [kəˈnuː].

[uə] halboffenes halblanges u mit nachhallendem ə: *poor* [puə], *sure* [ʃuə], *allure* [əˈljuə].

[u] flüchtiges u: *put* [put], *look* [luk], *careful* [ˈkɛəful].

Ganz vereinzelt werden auch die folgenden französischen Laute gebraucht: Die Nasale [ɑ̃] wie in frz. *blanc*, [ɔ̃] wie in frz. *bonbon* und [ɛ̃] wie in frz. *vin*, sowie die drei Vokale [o] wie in frz. *chaud*, [ɛ] wie in frz. *belle* und [ø] wie in frz. *monsieur*.

Die **Länge eines Vokals** wird durch [ː] bezeichnet, z. B. *ask* [ɑːsk], *astir* [əˈstəː]. Die **Betonung** der englischen Wörter wird durch das Zeichen [ˈ] vor der zu betonenden Silbe angegeben, z. B. *onion* [ˈʌnjən].

B. Konsonanten

[r] nur vor Vokalen gesprochen. Völlig verschieden vom deutschen Zungenspitzen- oder Zäpfchen-r. Die Zungenspitze bildet mit der oberen Zahnwulst eine Enge, durch die der Ausatmungsstrom mit Stimmton hindurchgetrieben wird, ohne den Laut zu rollen. Am Ende eines Wortes wird r nur bei Bindung mit dem Anlautvokal des folgenden Wortes gesprochen: *rose* [rəuz], *pride* [praid], *there is* [ðɛərˈiz].

[ʒ] stimmhaftes sch, wie g in Genie, j in Journal: *azure* [ˈæʒə], *jazz* [dʒæz], *jeep* [dʒiːp], *large* [lɑːdʒ].

[ʃ] stimmloses sch, wie im Deutschen Schnee, rasch: *shake* [ʃeik], *washing* [ˈwɔʃiŋ], *lash* [læʃ].

[θ] im Deutschen nicht vorhandener stimmloser Lispellaut; durch Anlegen der Zunge an die oberen Schneidezähne hervorgebracht: *thin* [θin], *path* [pɑːθ], *method* [ˈmeθəd].

[ð] derselbe Laut stimmhaft, d. h. mit Stimmton: *there* [ðɛə], *breathe* [briːð], *father* [ˈfɑːðə].

[s] stimmloser Zischlaut, entsprechend dem deutschen ß in Spaß, reißen: *see* [siː], *hats* [hæts], *decide* [diˈsaid].

[z] stimmhafter Zischlaut wie im Deutschen sausen: *zeal* [ziːl], *rise* [raiz], *horizon* [həˈraizn].

[ŋ] wird wie der deutsche Nasenlaut in fangen, singen gebildet: *ring* [riŋ], *singer* [ˈsiŋə].

[ŋk] derselbe Laut mit nachfolgendem k wie im Deutschen senken, Wink: *ink* [iŋk], *tinker* [ˈtiŋkə].

[w] flüchtiges, mit Lippe an Lippe gesprochenes w, aus der Mundstellung für uː gebildet: *will* [wil], *swear* [swɛə], *queen* [kwiːn].

[f] stimmloser Lippenlaut wie im Deutschen flott: *fat* [fæt], *tough* [tʌf], *effort* [ˈefət].

[v] stimmhafter Lippenlaut wie im Deutschen Vase, Ventil: *vein* [vein], *velvet* [ˈvelvit].

[j] flüchtiger zwischen j und i schwebender Laut: *onion* [ˈʌnjən], *yes* [jes], *filial* [ˈfiljəl].

Verwandte Abkürzungen

o	vor einem englischen Wort im Text zeigt an, daß dieses Wort in der Vokabelspalte übersetzt wird.
Abkzg	Abkürzung
AE	amerikanisches Englisch
BE	britisches Englisch
F	Familiär (= Umgangssprache)
Pl	Plural
	Slang
V	Vulgär

Die in diesem Buch enthaltenen Geschichten wurden mit Genehmigung der folgenden Verlage und Agenturen veröffentlicht:

A. P. Watt & Son und Mohrbooks Literary Agency für "The Fiery Wooing of Mordred" und "The Knightly Quest of Mervyn" von P. G. Wodehouse.

Intercontinental Literary Agency für "My Oedipus Complex" und "A Salesman's Romance" von Frank O'Connor.

Putnam & Co. Ltd für "As Joe Said" von Herbert Sutherland (aus der Sammlung "Pick of Today's Short Stories No. 9" edited by John Pudney).

The °Fiery °Wooing of Mordred

BY P. G. WODEHOUSE

THE °Pint of °Lager breathed heavily through his nose.

'Silly °fathead!' he said. 'Ash-trays in every °nook and °cranny of the room—ash-trays staring you in the eye wherever you look—and he has to go and do a fool thing like that.'

He was °alluding to a young gentleman with a °vacant, fish-like face who, °leaving the °bar-parlour of the Anglers' Rest a few moments before, had thrown his cigarette into the °waste-paper-basket, °causing it to °burst into a cheerful °blaze. °Not one of the little company of amateur fire-fighters °but was °ruffled. A °Small °Bass with a high °blood pressure had had to have his °collar °loosened, and the °satin-clad °bosom of Miss Postlethwaite, our °emotional barmaid, was still °heaving.

Only Mr Mulliner seemed °disposed to take a tolerant view of what had °occurred.

°'In fairness to the lad,' he pointed out, °sipping his hot Scotch and lemon, 'we must remember that our bar-parlour contains no grand piano or °priceless old walnut table, which to the younger generation are the normal and natural °repositories for lighted cigarette-ends. °Failing these, he, of course, °selected the waste-paper-basket. Like Mordred.'

'Like who?' asked a °Whisky and °Splash.

fiery ['faiəri] *feurig*
wooing ['wu:iŋ] *das Werben (um eine Frau)*
pint [paint] *Hohlmaß (0,56 l)*
lager ['lɑ:gə] *Lagerbier*
a Pint of Lager, a Small Bass, a Whisky and Splash, etc. *scherzhafte Bezeichnung des Mannes nach dem, was er trinkt*
fathead ['fæthed] *Schafskopf*
nook [nuk] *Winkel, Ecke*
cranny ['kræni] *Spalte*
allude to [ə'lu:d] *anspielen auf*
vacant ['veikənt] *leer*
leave [li:v] *verlassen*
bar-parlour ['bɑ:'pɑ:lə] *Schankzimmer*
waste-paper-basket [weist-'peipəbɑ:skit] *Papierkorb*
cause [kɔ:z] *verursachen*
burst [bə:st] *bersten, ausbrechen*
blaze [bleiz] *hellodernde Flamme*
not one ... but was *nicht einer, der nicht ... gewesen wäre*
ruffled ['rʌfld] *verärgert, verstimmt*
Bass [bæs] *engl. Biermarke*
blood pressure ['blʌdpreʃə] *Blutdruck*
collar ['kɔlə] *Kragen*
loosen ['lu:sn] *lockern*
satin-clad ['sætinklæd] *in Seide gehüllt*
bosom ['buzəm] *Busen*
emotional [i'məuʃənl] *gefühlvoll, rührselig*
heave [hi:v] *(sich) heben*
disposed [dis'pəuzd] *geneigt*
occur [ə'kə:] *vorkommen, geschehen*
in fairness to the lad ['fɛənis] *um dem Jungen gerecht zu werden*
sip [sip] *schlürfen*
priceless ['praislis] *unbezahlbar*

'Whom,' corrected Miss Postlethwaite.

The Whisky and Splash apologized.

'A nephew of mine. Mordred Mulliner, the poet.'

'Mordred,' murmured Miss Postlethwaite °pensively. 'A sweet name.'

'And one,' said Mr Mulliner, 'that fitted him admirably, for he was a °comely lovable sensitive youth with large, °fawn-like eyes, °delicately °chiselled °features, and excellent teeth. I mention these teeth, because it was owing to them that °the train of events started which I °am about to describe.'

'He °bit somebody?' °queried Miss Postlethwaite, °groping.

'No. But if he had had no teeth he would not have gone to the dentist's that day, and if he had not gone to the dentist's he would not have met Annabelle.'

'Annabelle whom?'

'Who,' corrected Miss Postlethwaite.

°'Oh, shoot,' said the Whisky and Splash.

'Annabelle Sprockett-Sprockett, the only daughter of Sir Murgatroyd and Lady Sprockett-Sprockett of Smattering Hall, Worcestershire. Impractical in many ways,' said Mr Mulliner, 'Mordred never failed to visit his dentist every six months, and on the morning on which my story opens he had just seated himself in the empty waiting-room and was turning the pages of a three-months-old copy of the °*Tatler* when the door opened and there entered a girl at the sight of whom—or who, if our friend here prefers it—something seemed to explode on the left side of his

repository [ri'pɔzitəri] *Aufbewahrungsplatz*
failing these ['feiliŋ] *in deren Ermangelung*
select [si'lekt] *auswählen*
splash [splæʃ] *Spritzer*

---

pensively ['pensivli] *gedankenvoll*
comely ['kʌmli] *anmutig, hübsch*
fawn-like eyes ['fɔːnlaik] *Rehaugen (Vergleich)*
delicately ['delikitli] *zart*
chiselled ['tʃizld] *gemeißelt, wohlgeformt*
features ['fiːtʃəz] *Gesichtszüge*
the train of events [i'vents] *die Serie, (Reihe, Folge) von Ereignissen*
be about to [ə'baut] *im Begriffe sein zu*
bit [bit] *von* bite *beißen*
query ['kwiəri] *fragen*
grope [grəup] *(sich) herantasten*

Oh, shoot *sl.* [ʃuːt] *zum Teufel*

Tatler ['tætlə] *Name einer Zeitschrift*
tattler *Plauderer, Schwätzer*

chest like a bomb. The *Tatler* swam before his eyes, and when it °solidified again he realized that love had come to him at last.

Most of the Mulliners have fallen in love at first sight, but few with so good an excuse as Mordred. She was a singularly beautiful girl, and for a while it was this beauty of hers that °enchained my nephew's attention to the °exclusion of all else. It was only after he had sat °gulping for some minutes like a dog with a chicken bone in its throat that he detected the sadness in her face. He could see now that her eyes, as she °listlessly °perused her four-months-old copy of °***Punch***, were heavy with pain.

His heart °ached for her, and as there is something about the atmosphere of a dentist's waiting-room which breaks down the barriers of conventional etiquette °he was emboldened to speak.

'Courage!' he said. 'It may not be so bad, after all. He may just °fool about with that little mirror thing of his, and decide that there is nothing that needs to be done.'

For the first time she smiled—faintly, but °with sufficient breadth to give Mordred another powerful °jolt.

'I'm not worrying about the dentist,' she explained. 'My trouble is that I live miles away in the country and only get a chance of coming to London about twice a year for about a couple of hours. I was hoping that I should be able to °put in a long spell of window-shopping in Bond Street, but now I've got to wait °goodness knows how long. I don't suppose I shall have time to do a thing. My train goes at one-fifteen.'

solidify [sɔ'lidifai] *feste Form annehmen*

enchain [in'tʃein] *fesseln*
exclusion [iks'klu:ʒən] *Ausschluß*
gulp [gʌlp] *mühsam schlucken, würgen*

listlessly ['listlisli] *teilnahmslos*
peruse [pə'ru:z] *durchlesen*
Punch [pʌnʃ] *Name einer Zeitschrift*
punch *Kasperle, Hanswurst*
ache [eik] *schmerzen*

he was emboldened [im'bəuldənd] *er erkühnte sich*

fool about [fu:l] *herumspielen*

with sufficient breadth [sə'fiʃənt, bredθ] *hier: deutlich genug*
jolt [dʒəult] *Ruck, Anstoß*

put in a long spell of window-shopping *sich eine ganze Weile dem Schaufensterbummel widmen*

goodness knows ['gudnis] *der Himmel weiß*

All the °chivalry in Mordred came to the °surface like a °leaping °trout.

'If you would care to take my place—'

'Oh, I couldn't.'

'Please. I shall enjoy waiting. It will give me an opportunity of °catching up with my reading.'

'Well, if you really wouldn't mind—'

Considering that Mordred by this time °was in the market to °tackle dragons °on her behalf or to climb the loftiest peak of the Alps to supply her with edelweiss, he was able to assure her that he did not mind. So in she went, flashing at him a shy glance of °gratitude which nearly °doubled him up, and he lit a cigarette and fell into a reverie. And presently she came out and he sprang to his feet, °courteously throwing his cigarette into the waste-paper-basket.

She °uttered a cry. Mordred recovered the cigarette.

'Silly of me,' he said, with a °deprecating laugh. 'I'm always doing that. Absent-minded. I've burned two flats already this year.'

She caught her breath.

'Burned them to the ground?'

'Well, not to the ground. They were on the top floor.'

'But you burned them?'

'Oh, yes. I burned them.'

'Well, well!' She seemed to °muse. 'Well, good-bye, Mr—'

'Mulliner. Mordred Mulliner.'

'Good-bye, Mr Mulliner, and thank you so much.'

'Not at all, Miss—'

'Sprockett-Sprockett.'

chivalry ['ʃivəlri] *Ritterlichkeit*
surface ['səːfis] *Oberfläche*
leap [liːp] *springen*
trout [traut] *Forelle*

catch up with [kætʃ] *einholen, hier: nachholen (Lesestoff)*

be in the market ['mɑːkit] *auf dem Markt sein, hier: bereit sein*
tackle ['tækl] *in Angriff nehmen*
on her behalf [bi'hɑːf] *ihretwegen*
gratitude ['grætitjuːd] *Dankbarkeit*
double up F ['dʌbl] *„erledigen"*
courteously ['kəːtjəsli] *höflich*

utter ['ʌtə] *äußern, ausstoßen*
deprecating ['deprikeitiŋ] *geringschätzig*

muse [mjuːz] *sinnen, grübeln*

'Not at all, Miss Sprockett-Sprockett. A pleasure.'

She passed from the room, and a few minutes later he was lying back in the dentist's chair, filled with an °infinite sadness. This was not due to any activity on the part of the dentist, who had just said with a °rueful °sigh that there didn't seem to be anything to do this time, but to the fact that his life was now a °blank. He loved this beautiful girl, and he would never see her more. It was just another case of °ships that pass in the waiting-room.

°Conceive his astonishment, therefore, when by the afternoon post next day he received a letter which ran as follows:

'Smattering Hall,
'Lower Smattering-on-the-Wissel,
'Worcestershire.

'Dear Mr Mulliner,

'My little girl has told me how very kind you were to her at the dentist's today. I cannot tell you how grateful she was. She does so love to walk down Bond Street and breathe on the jewellers' windows, and but for you she would have had to go another six months without her little °treat.

'I suppose you are a very busy man, like everybody in London, but if you can spare the time it would give my husband and myself so much pleasure if you could run down and stay with us for a few days—a long week-end, or even longer if you can manage it.

'With best wishes,
'Yours sincerely,
'Aurelia Sprockett-Sprockett.'

infinite ['infinit] *grenzenlos*

rueful ['ru:ful] *traurig*
sigh [sai] *Seufzer*
blank [blæŋk] *Leere*
ships that pass [pɑ:s] *Schiffe, die aneinander vorüberfahren (Vergleich: Menschen, die aneinander vorbeigehen)*
conceive [kən'si:v] *sich etwas denken od. vorstellen*

treat [tri:t] *Hochgenuß, Vergnügen*

Mordred read this communication six times in a minute and a quarter and then seventeen times rather more slowly in order to °savour any *nuance* of it that he might have overlooked. He took it that the girl must have got his address from the dentist's secretary on her way out, and he was doubly °thrilled —first, by this °evidence that one so lovely was as intelligent as she was beautiful, and secondly because the whole thing seemed to him so frightfully °significant. A girl, he meant to say, does not get her mother to invite fellows to her country home for long week-ends (or even longer if they can manage it) unless such fellows have °made a pretty substantial hit with her. This, he °contended, stood to reason.

He hastened to the nearest post office, °dispatched a telegram to Lady Sprockett-Sprockett assuring her that he would be with her on the morrow, and returned to his flat to pack °his effects. His heart was singing within him. Apart from anything else, the invitation could not have come at a more fortunate moment, for what with musing on his great love while smoking cigarettes he had practically °gutted his little nest on the °previous evening, and while it was still °habitable in a sense there was no °gainsaying the fact that all those °charred sofas and things °struck a rather melancholy note and he would be glad to be away from it all for a few days.

It seemed to Mordred, as he travelled down on the following afternoon, that the wheels of the train, °clattering over

savour ['seivə] *auskosten*
thrilled [θrild] *aufgewühlt*
evidence ['evidəns] *Beweis*
significant [sig'nifikənt] *bedeutungsvoll*
make a hit [hit] *einen Treffer erzielen, Erfolg haben*
contend [kən'tend] *behaupten*
dispatch [dis'pætʃ] *absenden, aufgeben*
his effects [i'fekts] *seine bewegliche Habe, hier: seine Sachen*
gut [gʌt] *ausbrennen*
previous ['pri:vjəs] *vorhergehend*
habitable ['hæbitəbl] *bewohnbar*
gainsay ['geinsei] *bestreiten*
charred [tʃɑ:d] *angekohlt*
strike a note [straik] *einen Ton anschlagen, eine Stimmung heraufbeschwören*
clatter ['klætə] *rattern*

the metals, were singing 'Sprockett-Sprockett'—not 'Annabelle', of course, for he did not yet know her name—and it was with a whispered 'Sprockett-Sprockett' on his lips that he alighted at the little station of Smattering-cum-Blimpstead-in-the-Vale, which, as his °hostess's °note-paper had informed him, was where you got off for the Hall. And when he °perceived that the girl herself had come to meet him in a two-seater car the whisper nearly became a shout.

hostess ['həustis] *Gastgeberin*
note-paper ['nəutpeipə] *Briefpapier*
perceive [pə'si:v] *wahrnehmen*

For perhaps three minutes, as he sat beside her, Mordred remained in this condition of ecstatic °bliss. Here he was, he °reflected, and here she was—here, in fact, they both were—together, and he was just about to point out how jolly this was and—if he could work it without seeming to °rush things too much—to °drop a hint °to the effect that he could wish this state of affairs to continue through all eternity, when the girl drew up outside a tobacconist's.

bliss [blis] *Seligkeit*
reflect [ri'flekt] *überlegen*
rush things too much [rʌʃ] *die Sache überstürzen*
drop a hint [drɔp, hint] *eine Andeutung fallenlassen*
to the effect [i'fekt] *dem Sinne nach*

'I won't be a minute,' she said. 'I promised Biffy I would bring him back some cigarettes.'

A cold hand seemed to lay itself on Mordred's heart.

'Biffy?'

'Captain Biffing, one of the men at the Hall. And Guffy wants some pipe-cleaners.'

'Guffy?'

'Jack Guffington. I expect you know his name, if you are interested in °racing. He was third in last year's Grand National.'

racing ['reisiŋ] *Rennsport*

'Is he staying at the Hall, too?'

'Yes.'

'You have a large house-party?'

'Oh, not so very. Let me see. There's Billy Biffing, Jack Guffington, Ted Prosser, Freddie Boot—he's the tennis champion of the county—Tommy Mainprice, and—oh, yes, Algy Fripp —the °big-game hunter, you know.'

The hand on Mordred's heart, now definitely iced, tightened its grip. With a lover's °sanguine optimism, he had supposed that this visit of his was going to be just three days of jolly °sylvan solitude with Annabelle Sprockett-Sprockett. And now it appeared that the place was unwholesomely crowded with his fellow men. And what fellow men! Big-game hunters... Tennis champions ... Chaps who rode in Grand Nationals ... He could see them in his mind's eye—°lean, °wiry, °riding-breeched and °flannel-trousered young Apollos, °any one of them capable of cutting out his weight in Clark Gables.

A faint hope stirred within him.

'You have also, of course, with you Mrs Biffing, Mrs Guffington, Mrs Prosser, Mrs Boot, Mrs Mainprice, and Mrs Algernon Fripp?'

'Oh, no, they aren't married.'

'None of them?'

'No.'

The faint hope °coughed quietly and died.

'Ah,' said Mordred.

While the girl was in the shop, he remained °brooding. The fact that not one of these °blisters should be married filled him with an °austere °disapproval. If they had had the least °spark of °civic sense, he felt, they would have taken on the duties and °responsibilities of °matrimony years ago. But no. °Intent upon

big-game hunter [geim, 'hʌntə] *Großwildjäger*
sanguine ['sæŋgwin] *zuversichtlich; lebhaft*
sylvan solitude ['silvən 'sɔlitju:d] *Waldeseinsamkeit*

lean [li:n] mager
wiry ['waiəri] *drahtig*
riding-breeched ['raidiŋ-britʃt] *mit Reithosen bekleidet*
flannel-trousered ['flænl-trauzəd] *mit leichten Wollhosen bekleidet*
any ... cutting out his weight in Clark Gables [weit, klɑ:k 'geiblz] *jeder von ihnen könnte sich mit den Filmgrößen wie Cl. G. erfolgreich messen*

cough [kɔf] *husten*
brood [bru:d] *(vor sich hin)-brüten*
blisters *sl.* ['blistəz] *aufgeblasene Kerle*
austere [ɔs'tiə] *streng*
disapproval [disə'pru:vəl] *Mißbilligung*
spark [spɑ:k] *Funken*
civic ['sivik] *(staats)bürgerlich*
responsibility [rispɔnsə'biliti] *Verantwortung*
matrimony ['mætriməni] *Ehestand*
intent upon [in'tent] *erpicht auf*

their selfish pleasures, they had °callously remained bachelors. It was this spirit of °*laissez-faire*, Mordred considered, that was eating like a °canker into the soul of England.

He °was aware of Annabelle standing beside him.

'Eh?' he said, starting.

'I was saying: "Have you plenty of cigarettes?"'

'Plenty, thank you.'

'Good. And of course there will be a box in your room. Men always like to smoke in their bedrooms, don't they? As a matter of fact, two boxes—Turkish and Virginian. Father put them there specially.'

'Very kind of him,' said Mordred mechanically.

He °relapsed into a °moody silence, and they drove off.

It would be agreeable (said Mr Mulliner) if, having shown you my nephew so gloomy, so °apprehensive, so °tortured with dark °forebodings at this °juncture, I were able now to state that the hearty English welcome of Sir Murgatroyd and Lady Sprockett-Sprockett on his arrival at the Hall cheered him up and put new life into him. Nothing, too, would give me greater pleasure than to say that he found, on °encountering the °dreaded Biffies and Guffies, that they were negligible little °runts with faces incapable of inspiring affection in any good woman.

But I must °adhere °rigidly to the facts. °Genial, even °effusive, though his °host and hostess showed themselves, their °cordiality left him cold. And, so

callously ['kæləsli] *verhärtet, gefühllos*
laissez-faire ['leisei'fɛə] *sich gehen lassen*
canker ['kæŋkə] *Krebsgeschwür*
be aware of s.th. [ə'wɛə] *sich einer Sache bewußt sein*

relapse [ri'læps] *zurückfallen*
moody ['mu:di] *mißgestimmt, düster*

apprehensive [æpri'hensiv] *empfindsam*
tortured ['tɔ:tʃəd] *gequält*
forebodings [fɔ:'bəudiŋz] *Vorahnungen*
juncture ['dʒʌŋktʃə] *hier: Zeitpunkt*

encounter [in'kauntə] *begegnen*
dreaded ['dredid] *gefürchtet, furchtbar*
runt F [rʌnt] *lächerlicher Zwerg*
adhere to [əd'hiə] *sich halten an*
rigidly ['ridʒidli] *streng*
genial ['dʒi:njəl] *herzlich*
effusive [i'fju:siv] *überschwenglich*
host [həust] *Gastgeber*
cordiality [kɔ:di'æliti] *Herzlichkeit*

far from his rivals being °weeds, they were one and all models of manly beauty, and the spectacle of their °obvious °worship of Annabelle cut my nephew like a knife.

And on top of all this there was Smattering Hall itself.

Smattering Hall °destroyed Mordred's last hope. It was one of those °vast °edifices, so common throughout the countryside of England, whose °original °founders seem to have °budgeted for families of twenty-five or so and a domestic staff of not less than a hundred. 'Home isn't home,' one can picture them saying to themselves, 'unless you have plenty of elbow room.' And so this huge, majestic °pile had come into being. Romantic persons, confronted with it, thought of °knights in armour riding forth to the °Crusades. More °earthy individuals felt that it must cost a packet to keep up. Mordred's reaction on passing through the front door was a sort of sick sensation, a kind of °settled despair.

How, he asked himself, even °assuming that by some miracle he succeeded in fighting his way to her heart through all these Biffies and Guffies, could he ever dare to take Annabelle from a home like this? He had quite °satisfactory private °means, of course, and would be able, when married, to give up the bachelor flat and spread himself to something on a bigger °scale—possibly, if °sufficiently °*bijou*, even a °desirable residence in the Mayfair district. But after Smattering Hall would not Annabelle feel like a sardine in the largest of London houses?

weed [wi:d] *Unkraut, hier: schwächlicher Kümmerling*
obvious ['ɔbviəs] *offensichtlich*
worship ['wə:ʃip] *Verehrung*

destroy [dis'trɔi] *zerstören*
vast [vɑ:st] *riesig, ungeheuer*
edifice ['edifis] *Gebäude*
original [ə'ridʒənl] *ursprünglich*
founder ['faundə] *Gründer*
budget for ['bʌdʒit] *hier: vorsehen od. berechnen für*

pile [pail] *großes Gebäude, Gebäudekomplex*
knight in armour [nait in 'ɑ:mə] *Ritter in Rüstung*
Crusade [kru:'seid] *Kreuzzug*
earthy ['ə:θi] *materiell gesinnt*

settled despair ['setld dis'pɛə] *stille Verzweiflung*
assume [ə'sju:m] *annehmen*

satisfactory [sætis'fæktəri] *zufriedenstellend*
means [mi:nz] *(Geld)Mittel, Vermögen*
scale [skeil] *Maßstab*
sufficiently [sə'fiʃəntli] *hinreichend*
bijou ['bi:ʒu:] *klein und elegant*
desirable [di'zaiərəbl] *begehrenswert; angenehm*

Such were the dark thoughts that raced through Mordred's °brain before, during and after dinner. At eleven o'clock he °pleaded °fatigue after his journey, and Sir Murgatroyd accompanied him to his room, anxious, like a good host, to see that everything was comfortable.

'Very sensible of you to °turn in early,' he said, in his °bluff, genial way. 'So many young men ruin their health with late hours. Now you, I imagine, will just get into a °dressing-gown and smoke a cigarette or two and have the light out by twelve. You have plenty of cigarettes? I told them to see that you were well supplied. I always think the bedroom smoke is the best one of the day. Nobody to °disturb you, and all that. If you want to write letters or anything, there is lots of paper, and here is the waste-paper-basket, which is always so necessary. Well, good night, my boy, good night.'

The door closed, and Mordred, as °foreshadowed, got into a dressing-gown and lit a cigarette. But though, having done this, he made his way to the writing-table, it was not with any idea of °getting abreast of his correspondence. It was his purpose to compose a poem to Annabelle Sprockett-Sprockett. He had felt it °seething within him all the evening, and sleep would be impossible °until it was out of his °system.

°Hitherto, I should mention, my nephew's poetry, for he belonged to the modern fearless school, had always been °stark and rhymeless and had °dealt °principally with °corpses and the smell of cooking °cabbage. But now,

brain [brein] *Gehirn, hier: Kopf*
plead [pli:d] *geltend machen*
fatigue [fə'ti:g] *Übermüdung, Erschöpfung*

turn in [tə:n] *sich niederlegen, zu Bett gehen*
bluff [blʌf] *rauhbeinig, derb*
dressing-gown ['dresiŋgaun] *Schlafrock*

disturb [dis'tə:b] *stören*

foreshadow [fɔ:'ʃædəu] *ankündigen*

get abreast of [ə'brest] *nachkommen mit, Rückstände aufarbeiten*

seethe [si:ð] *kochen, gären*
system ['sistim] Organismus
until it was out of his system *bis er es draußen hatte*
hitherto ['hiðətu:] *bis dahin*
stark [stɑ:k] *hier: sachlich*
dealt with [delt] *von* deal with *handeln von*
principally ['prinsəpli] *hauptsächlich*
corpse [kɔ:ps] *Leiche*
cabbage ['kæbidʒ] *Kohl*

with the moonlight silvering the balcony outside, he found that his mind had become full of words like 'love' and °'dove' and 'eyes' and 'summer skies'.

Blue eyes, wrote Mordred ...
Sweet lips, wrote Mordred ...
Oh, *eyes like skies of summer blue* ...
Oh, *love* ...
Oh, *dove* ...
Oh, *lips* ...

With a °muttered °ejaculation of °chagrin he tore the sheet across and threw it into the waste-paper-basket.

Blue eyes that burn into my soul,
Sweet lips that smile my heart away,
°Pom-pom, pom-pom, pom something whole (°Goal?)
And °tiddly-iddly-umpty-ay (Gay? Say? Happy day?)

Blue eyes into my soul that burn,
Sweet lips that smile away my heart,
Oh, something something turn or °yearn
And something something something part.

You burn into my soul, blue eyes,
You smile my heart away, sweet lips,
Short long short long of summer skies
And something something something °trips. (°Hips? Ships? °Pips?)

He °threw the sheet into the waste-paper-basket and °rose with a °stifled °oath. The waste-paper-basket was nearly full now, and still his poet's sense told him that he had not °achieved perfection. He thought he saw the reason for this. You can't just sit in a chair and

dove [dʌv] *Taube*

mutter ['mʌtə] *murmeln*
ejaculation [idʒækju'leiʃən] *Ausruf*
chagrin ['ʃægrin] *Ärger*

goal [gəul] *Ziel*
pom-pom, tiddly-iddly-umpty-ay *sinnlose Füllsel, mit denen der „Dichter" die noch leeren Stellen ausfüllt*

yearn [jə:n] *sich sehnen*

trip [trip] *stolpern*
hip [hip] *Hüfte*
pip [pip] *(kleiner) Obstkern*
threw [θru:] *von* throw *werfen*
rose [rəuz] *von* rise *aufstehen*
stifle ['staifl] *unterdrücken*
oath [əuθ] *Eid, hier: Fluch*
achieve [ə'tʃi:v] *erreichen, vollbringen*

expect inspiration to flow—you want to walk about and °clutch your hair and °snap your fingers. It had been his intention to pace the room, but the moonlight pouring in through the open window called to him. He went out on to the balcony. It was but a short distance to the °dim, mysterious lawn. Impulsively he dropped from the stone balustrade.

The effect °was magical. °Stimulated by the improved conditions, his Muse gave quick service, and this time he saw at once that she had rung the bell and delivered the goods. One turn up and down the lawn, and he was reciting as follows:

TO ANNABELLE

Oh, lips that smile! Oh, eyes that
shine
Like summer skies, or stars above!
Your beauty °maddens me like wine,
Oh, umpty-pumpty-tumty love!

And he was just wondering, for he was a severe critic of his own work, whether that last line couldn't be polished up a bit, when his eye was attracted by something that shone like summer skies or stars above and, looking more closely, he perceived that his bedroom curtains were on fire.

Now, I will not pretend that my nephew Mordred was in every respect the cool-headed man of action, but this happened to be a situation with which use had °familiarized him. He knew the °procedure.

'Fire!' he shouted.

clutch [klʌtʃ] *(krampfhaft) packen*
snap one's fingers [snæp] *mit den Fingern schnalzen*

dim [dim] *düster*
was magical ['mædʒikəl] *hier: grenzte ans Wunderbare*
stimulate ['stimjuleit] *anregen*

madden ['mædn] *verrückt machen*

familiarize [fə'miljəraiz] *vertraut machen*
procedure [prə'si:dʒə] *Vorgang*

A head appeared in an upstairs window. He recognized it as that of Captain Biffing.

'Eh?' said Captain Biffing.

'Fire!'

'What?'

'Fire!' °vociferated Mordred. 'F for Francis, I for Isabel ...'

'Oh, fire?' said Captain Biffing. 'Right ho.'

And presently the house began to °discharge its °occupants.

In the °proceedings which followed, Mordred, I fear, did not appear to the greatest advantage. This is an age of specialization, and if you take the specialist off his own °particular ground he °is at a loss. Mordred's genius, as we have seen, lay in the direction of starting fires. Putting them out called for quite different qualities, and these he did not possess. On the various occasions of °holocausts at his series of flats, he had never °attempted to play an active part, °contenting himself with going downstairs and asking the °janitor to step up and see what he could do about it. So now, though under the bright eyes of Annabelle Sprockett-Sprockett he would have given much to be able to °dominate the scene, the truth is that the Biffies and Guffies simply °played him off the stage.

His heart sank as he noted the °hideous °efficiency of these young men. They called for °buckets. They formed a line. Freddie Boot °leaped °lissomely on to the balcony, and Algy Fripp, °mounted on a wheelbarrow, handed up to him the necessary °supplies. And after Mordred, trying to do his bit, had

vociferate [vəu'sifəreit] *brüllen*

discharge [dis'tʃɑ:dʒ] *(sich) entladen, von sich geben, hier: ausspeien*
occupant ['ɔkjupənt] *Insasse*
proceedings [prə'si:diŋz] *hier: Maßnahmen*
particular [pə'tikjulə] *besonder*
be at a loss [lɔs] *versagen; hilflos od. in Verlegenheit sein*

holocaust ['hɔləkɔ:st] *Brandkatastrophe*
attempt [ə'tempt] *versuchen*
content oneself with [kən'tent] *sich zufriedengeben mit*
janitor ['dʒænitə] *Portier, Hausmeister*

dominate ['dɔmineit] *beherrschen*
play s.o. off the stage [steidʒ] *j-n an die Wand spielen*
hideous ['hidiəs] *abscheulich*
efficiency [i'fiʃənsi] *Tüchtigkeit*
bucket ['bʌkit] *Eimer*
leap [li:p] *springen*
lissomely ['lisəmli] *geschmeidig, gewandt*
mount [maunt] *besteigen*
mounted on ... *hier: auf ... stehend*

supplies *Pl* [sə'plaiz] *Vorrat, Versorgung, hier: Material*

°tripped up Jack Guffington and °upset two buckets over Ted Prosser, °he was advised in set terms to °withdraw into the background and stay there.

It was a black ten minutes for the unfortunate young man. One glance at Sir Murgatroyd's °twisted face as he watched the °operations was enough to tell him how desperately anxious the fine old man was for the safety of °his ancestral home and how bitter would be his °resentment against the person who had °endangered it. And the same °applied to Lady Sprockett-Sprockett and Annabelle. Mordred could see the anxiety in their eyes, and the thought that °ere long those eyes must be turned °accusingly on him °chilled him to the °marrow.

trip up [trip] *zum Stolpern bringen*
upset [ʌp'set] *umstürzen*
he was advised in set terms [əd'vaizd] *man riet ihm unmißverständlich*
withdraw [wið'drɔː] *(sich) zurückziehen*
twist [twist] *verzerren*
operation [ɔpə'reiʃən] *Handlung, Vorgang*
his ancestral home [æn'sestrəl] *das Haus seiner Ahnen*
resentment [ri'zentmənt] *Groll*
endanger [in'deindʒə] *gefährden*
apply to [ə'plai] *gelten für, anwenden auf*
ere long [ɛə] *bald*
accusingly [ə'kjuːziŋli] *anklagend*
chill s.o. [tʃil] *j-n frösteln lassen*
marrow ['mærəu] *(das) Mark*

Presently Freddie Boot °emerged from the bedroom to announce that all was well.

emerge [i'məːdʒ] *auftauchen*

'It's out,' he said, jumping lightly down. 'Anybody know whose room it was?'

Mordred felt a °sickening °qualm, but the °splendid Mulliner courage °sustained him. He stepped forward, white and °tense.

'Mine,' he said.

He became the °instant centre of attention. The six young men looked at him.

'Yours?'

'Oh, yours, was it?'

'What happened?'

'How did it start?'

'Yes, how did it start?'

'Must have started somehow, I mean,' said Captain Biffing, who was a

sickening ['sikniŋ] *ekelhaft, gräßlich*
qualm [kwɑːm] *Übelkeit*
splendid ['splendid] *prächtig*
sustain [səs'tein] *aufrecht halten*
tense [tens] *angespannt*
instant ['instənt] *augenblicklich*

clear thinker. 'I mean to say, must have, don't you know, what?'

Mordred mastered his voice.

'I was smoking, and I suppose I threw my cigarette into the waste-paper-basket, and as it was full of paper ...'

'Full of paper? Why was it full of paper?'

'I had been writing a poem.'

There was a °stir of bewilderment.

'A what?' said Ted Prosser.

'Writing a what?' said Jack Guffington.

'Writing a *poem*?' asked Captain Biffing of Tommy Mainprice.

'That's how I got the story,' said Tommy Mainprice, °plainly °shaken.

°'Chap was writing a poem,' Freddie Boot informed Algy Fripp.

'You mean the chap writes poems?'

'That's right. Poems.'

'Well, °I'm dashed!'

'Well, °I'm blowed!'

Their now °unconcealed °scorn was hard to bear. Mordred °chafed beneath it. The word 'poem' was °flitting from lip to lip, and it was only too evident that, had there been an 's' in the word, those present would have °hissed it. Reason told him that these men were °mere °clods, Philistines, fatheads who would not recognize the rare and the beautiful if you handed it to them on a °skewer, but that did not seem to make it any better. He knew that he should be scorning them, but it is not easy to go about scorning people in a dressing-gown, especially if you have no socks on and the night breeze is cool around the °ankles. So, as I say, he chafed. And finally, when he saw the butler °bend

stir [stəː] *Bewegung*

plainly ['pleinli] *offensichtlich*
shaken ['ʃeikən] *erschüttert*
chap [tʃæp] *Bursche, Kerl*

I'm dashed! *sl.* [dæʃt] *Verdammt!*
I'm blowed! *sl.* [bləud] *Mir bleibt die Spucke weg!*
unconcealed ['ʌnkən'siːld] *unverhohlen*
scorn [skɔːn] *Verachtung*
chafe [tʃeif] *wüten, toben*
flit [flit] *flitzen*
hiss [his] *zischen*

mere [miə] *bloß, nichts als*
clod [klɔd] *Erdklumpen, hier: Tölpel*
skewer ['skjuːə] *Spieß*

ankle [æŋkl] *Fußknöchel*
bend down [bend] *sich neigen, bücken*

down with °pursed lips to the ear of the cook, who was a little hard of hearing, and after a °contemptuous °glance in his direction speak into it, °spacing his syllables carefully, something within him seemed to snap.

'I regret, Sir Murgatroyd,' he said, 'that urgent family business °compels me to return to London immediately. I shall be obliged to take the first train in the morning.'

Without another word he went into the house.

purse one's lips [pə:s] *den Mund spitzen*
contemptuous [kən'temptjuəs] *verächtlich*
glance [glɑ:ns] *Blick*
space [speis] *hier: artikulieren*
compel [kəm'pel] *zwingen*

In the matter of camping out in °devastated areas my nephew had, of course, become by this time °an old hand. It was rarely nowadays that a few ashes and °cinders about the place disturbed him. But when he had returned to his bedroom one look was enough to assure him that nothing practical in the way of sleep was to be achieved here. Apart from the unpleasant, °acrid smell of burned poetry, the apartment, thanks to the efforts of Freddie Boot, had been °converted into a kind of inland sea. The carpet was °awash, and on the bed only a duck could have made itself at home.

And so it came about that some ten minutes later Mordred Mulliner lay stretched upon a high-backed couch in the library, endeavouring by means of counting sheep jumping through a °gap in a hedge to °lull himself into unconsciousness.

But sleep °refused to come. Nor in his heart had he really thought that it would. When the human soul is on the °rack, it cannot just curl up and close

devastated ['devəsteitid] *verwüstet*
an old hand *ein alter Hase*
cinder ['sində] *Schlacke, hier: verkohlter Rest*
acrid ['eikrid] *scharf, beißend*
convert [kən'və:t] *verwandeln*
awash [ə'wɔʃ] *unter Wasser*
gap [gæp] *Lücke*
lull into unconsciousness [lʌl, ʌn'kɔnʃəsnis] *hier: einlullen*
refuse [ri'fju:z] *ablehnen, sich weigern*
rack [ræk] *Folter*

its eyes and expect to get its eight hours as if nothing had happened. It was all very well for Mordred to count sheep, but what did this profit him when each sheep in turn assumed the features and °lineaments of Annabelle Sprockett-Sprockett and, what was more, gave him a °reproachful glance as it drew itself together for the spring?

°Remorse °gnawed him. He was °tortured by a wild °regret for what might have been. He was not saying that with all these Biffies and Guffies in the field he had ever had more than a hundred to eight chance of winning that lovely girl, but at least °his hat had been in the ring. Now it was definitely out. Dreamy Mordred may have been —romantic—impractical—but he had enough sense to see that the very worst thing you can do when you are trying to make a °favourable impression on the °adored object is to set fire to her childhood home, every stick and stone of which she has no doubt worshipped since they put her into °rompers.

He had reached this point in his meditations, and was about to send his two hundred and thirty-second sheep at the gap, when with a suddenness which affected him much as an explosion of °gelignite would have done, the lights flashed on. For an instant, he lay °quivering, then, °cautiously °poking his head round the corner of the couch, he looked to see who his visitors were.

It was a little party of three that had entered the room. First came Sir Murgatroyd, carrying a °tray of sandwiches. He was followed by Lady Sprockett-Sprockett with a siphon and

lineaments ['linjəmənts] *hier: Umrisse*
reproachful [ri'prəutʃful] *vorwurfsvoll*
remorse [ri'mɔːs] *Reue*
gnaw [nɔː] *nagen (an)*
torture ['tɔːtʃə] *foltern, quälen*
regret [ri'gret] *Bedauern*

his hat had been in the ring F *er hätte sich zum Kampf gestellt*

favourable ['feivərəbl] *günstig*
adore [ə'dɔː] *anbeten*

rompers ['rɔmpəz] *Spielanzug*

gelignite ['dʒelignait] *Gelatinedynamit*
quiver ['kwivə] *zittern*
cautiously ['kɔːʃəsli] *vorsichtig*
poke [pəuk] *stecken*

tray [trei] *Tablett*

glasses. The rear was °brought up by Annabelle, who was bearing a bottle of whisky and two dry °ginger ales.

So evident was it that they were assembling here for purposes of a family council that, but for one circumstance, Mordred, to whom anything in the nature of °eavesdropping was as °repugnant as it has always been to all the Mulliners, would have sprung up with a polite 'Excuse me' and taken his blanket elsewhere. This circumstance was the fact that on lying down he had kicked his slippers under the couch, well out of reach. The soul of °modesty, he could not affront Annabelle with the spectacle of his bare toes.

So he lay there in silence, and silence, broken only by the swishing of soda-water and the *whoosh* of opened ginger-ale bottles, reigned in the room beyond.

Then Sir Murgatroyd spoke.

'Well, that's that,' he said, °bleakly.

There was a gurgle as Lady Sprockett-Sprockett drank ginger ale. Then her quiet, well-bred voice broke the pause.

'Yes,' she said, 'it is the end.'

'The end,' agreed Sir Murgatroyd heavily. 'No good trying to °struggle on against luck like ours. Here we are and here we have got to stay, °mouldering on in this °blasted °barrack of a place which eats up every penny of my income when, °but for the fussy °interference of that gang of °officious, ugly °nitwits, there would have been nothing left of it but a pile of ashes, with a man from the Insurance Company standing on it with his fountain-pen, writing cheques. Curse those °imbeciles! Did

brought up the rear [brɔːt, riə] *von* bring up... *die Nachhut bilden*
ginger ale [ˈdʒindʒəˈeil] *Ingwerbier*
eavesdropping [ˈiːvzdrɔpiŋ] *Horchen, Belauschen*
repugnant [riˈpʌgnənt] *abstoßend*
modesty [ˈmɔdisti] *Sittsamkeit; Bescheidenheit*
bleakly [ˈbliːkli] *frostig, freudlos*
struggle on [ˈstrʌgl] *weiterkämpfen*
moulder [ˈməuldə] *verschimmeln*
blasted [ˈblɑːstid] *hier: verdammt*
barrack [ˈbærək] *Baracke, Bude*
but for *wenn nicht ... gewesen wäre*
fussy [ˈfʌsi] *übertrieben geschäftig*
interference [intəˈfiərəns] *Einmischung*
officious [əˈfiʃəs] *aufdringlich*
nitwit [ˈnitwit] *Dummkopf*
imbecile [ˈimbisiːl] *Schwachsinnige*

you see that young Fripp with those buckets?'

'I did, indeed,' sighed Lady Sprockett-Sprockett.

'Annabelle,' said Sir Murgatroyd sharply.

'Yes, father?'

'It has seemed to me lately, watching you with a father's eye, that you have shown signs of being attracted by Algernon Fripp. Let me tell you that if ever you allow yourself to be °ensnared by his °insidious °wiles, or by those of William Biffing, John Guffington, Edward Prosser, Thomas Mainprice, or Frederick Boot, you will do so over my dead body. After what occurred tonight, those young men shall never darken my door again. They and their buckets! To think that we could have gone and lived in London ...'

'In a nice little flat ...' said Lady Sprockett-Sprockett.

°'Handy for my club ...'

'Convenient for the shops ...'

'Within a stone's throw of the theatres ...'

'Seeing all our friends ...'

'Had it not been,' said Sir Murgatroyd, summing up, 'for the °pestilential activities of these Guffingtons, these Biffings, these °insufferable Fripps, men who ought never to be trusted near a bucket of water when a °mortgaged country-house has got nicely alight. I did think,' °proceeded the °stricken old man, helping himself to a sandwich, 'that when Annabelle, with a ready intelligence which I cannot over-praise, realized this young Mulliner's splendid gifts and made us ask him down here,

ensnare [in'snεə] *in die Falle locken*
insidious [in'sidiəs] *hinterlistig*
wiles [wailz] *Ränke*

handy ['hændi] *bequem, leicht erreichbar*

pestilential [pesti'lenʃəl] *scheußlich, widerlich*
insufferable [in'sʌfərəbl] *unerträglich*
mortgaged ['mɔːgidʒd] *verpfändet, hypothekenbelastet*
proceed [prə'siːd] *fortfahren*
stricken ['strikən] *heimgesucht, geschlagen*

the happy ending was in sight. What Smattering Hall has needed for generations has been a man who throws his cigarette-ends into waste-paper-baskets. I was °convinced that here at last was the angel of °mercy we °required.'

'He did his best, father.'

'No man could have done more,' agreed Sir Murgatroyd cordially. 'The way he upset those buckets and kept getting °entangled in people's legs. Very °shrewd. It thrilled me to see him. I don't know when I've met a young fellow I liked and respected more. And what if he is a poet? Poets are all right. Why, dash it, I'm a poet myself. At the last dinner of the Loyal Sons of Worcestershire I composed a poem which, let me tell you, was pretty generally admired. I read it out to the boys over the °port, and they °cheered me to the echo. It was about a young lady of Bewdley, who sometimes behaved rather rudely ...'

'Not before mother, father.'

'Perhaps you're right. Well, I'm off to bed. Come along, Aurelia. You coming, Annabelle?'

'Not yet, father. I want to stay and think.'

'Do what?'

'Think.'

'Oh, think? Well, all right.'

'But, Murgatroyd,' said Lady Sprockett-Sprockett, 'is there no hope? After all, there are plenty of cigarettes in the house, and we could always give Mr Mulliner another waste-paper-basket. ...'

'No good. You heard him say he was leaving by the first train to-morrow. When I think that we shall never see

convince [kən'vins] *überzeugen*
mercy ['mə:si] *Gnade*
require [ri'kwaiə] *brauchen*

entangle [in'tæŋgl] *verwickeln*
shrewd [ʃru:d] *schlau*

port [pɔ:t] *Portwein*
cheer a person to the echo [tʃiə, 'ekəu] *j-m laut zujubeln*

that splendid young man again ... Why, hullo, hullo, hullo, what's this? Crying, Annabelle?'

'Oh, mother!'

'My darling, what is it?'

A °choking °sob escaped the girl.

'Mother, I love him! Directly I saw him in the dentist's waiting-room, something seemed to go all over me, and I knew that there could be no other man for me. And now ...'

'Hi!' cried Mordred, °popping up over the side of the couch like a °jack-in-the-box.

He had listened with growing understanding to the conversation which I have °related, but had °shrunk from °revealing his presence because, as I say, his toes were bare. But this was too much. Toes or no toes, he felt that he must be in this.

'You love me, Annabelle?' he cried.

His sudden °advent had °occasioned, I need scarcely say, a certain reaction in those present. Sir Murgatroyd had leaped like a °jumping bean. Lady Sprockett-Sprockett had quivered like a °jelly. As for Annabelle, her lovely mouth was open to the °extent of perhaps three inches, and she was staring like one who sees a vision.

'You really love me, Annabelle?'

'Yes, Mordred.'

'Sir Murgatroyd,' said Mordred formally, 'I have the honour to ask for your daughter's hand. I am only a poor poet ...'

'How poor?' asked the other, keenly.

'I was °referring to my art,' explained Mordred. 'Financially, I am nicely

choking ['tʃəukiŋ] *erstickt*
sob [sɔb] *Schluchzen*

pop up [pɔp] *plötzlich auftauchen*
jack-in-the-box [dʒæk] *Schachtelmännchen*

relate [ri'leit] *erzählen*
shrunk from [ʃrʌŋk] *von* shrink from *sich scheuen vor, zurückschrecken vor*
reveal [ri'vi:l] *offenbaren, kundtun*

advent ['ædvənt] *Erscheinen*
occasion [ə'keiʒən] *verursachen*
jumping bean ['dʒʌmpiŋbi:n] *(mexikanische) Springbohne*
jelly ['dʒeli] *Gelee*
extent [iks'tent] *Ausmaß, Größe*

refer to [ri'fə:] *sich beziehen auf*

fixed. I could support Annabelle in modest comfort.'

'Then take her, my boy, take her. You will live, of course'—the old man °winced— 'in London?'

'Yes. And so shall you.'

Sir Murgatroyd shook his head.

'No, no, that dream is ended. It is true that in certain circumstances I had hoped to do so, for the insurance, I may mention, amounts to as much as a hundred thousand pounds, but I °am resigned now to spending the rest of my life in this °infernal family °vault. I see no °reprieve.'

'I understand,' said Mordred, °nodding. 'You mean you have no °paraffin in the house?'

Sir Murgatroyd started.

'Paraffin?'

'If,' said Mordred, and his voice was very gentle and winning, 'there had been paraffin °on the premises, I think it possible that to-night's °conflagration, doubtless imperfectly °quenched, might have broken out again, this time with more serious results. It is often this way with fires. You pour buckets of water on them and think they are extinguished, but all the time they have been °smouldering unnoticed, to break out once more in—well, in here, for example.'

'Or the billiard-room,' said Lady Sprockett-Sprockett.

'*And* the billiard-room,' corrected Sir Murgatroyd.

'And the billiard-room,' said Mordred. 'And possibly—who knows?—in the drawing-room, dining-room, kitchen, servants' hall, butler's pantry and

wince [wins] *(zusammen)zukken*

be resigned to [ri'zaind] *sich abfinden mit*
infernal [in'fəːnl] *teuflisch*
vault [vɔːlt] *Gruft*
reprieve [ri'priːv] *Begnadigung*
nod [nɔd] *nicken*
paraffin ['pærəfin] *Paraffin*

on the premises ['premisiz] *an Ort und Stelle; hier: im Hause*
conflagration [kɔnflə'greiʃən] *Brand*
quench [kwentʃ] *löschen*

smoulder ['sməuldə] *schwelen*

the usual domestic offices, as well. Still, as you say you have no paraffin ...'

'My boy,' said Sir Murgatroyd, in a shaking voice, 'what gave you the idea that we have no paraffin? How did you fall into this odd error? We have °gallons of paraffin. The cellar is full of it.'

'And Annabelle will show you the way to the cellar—in case you thought of going there,' said Lady Sprockett-Sprockett. 'Won't you, dear?'

'Of course, mother. You will like the cellar, Mordred, darling. Most °picturesque. Possibly, if you are interested in paraffin, you might also care to take a look at our little store of paper and °shavings, too.'

'My angel,' said Mordred, tenderly, 'you think of everything.'

He found his slippers, and hand in hand they passed down the stairs. Above them, they could see the head of Sir Murgatroyd, as he leaned over the °banisters. A box of matches fell at their feet like a father's °benediction.

gallon ['gælən] *Gallone (4,541)*

picturesque [piktʃə'resk] *malerisch*

shavings ['ʃeiviŋz] *Späne, Schnitzel*

banisters *Pl* ['bænistəz] *Treppengeländer*

benediction [beni'dikʃən] *Segen*

The °Knightly °Quest of Mervyn

BY P. G. WODEHOUSE

SOME sort of smoking-concert seemed to be in progress in the large room across the °passage from the °bar-parlour of the °Anglers' Rest, and a music-loving °Stout and Mild had left the door open, °the better to enjoy the °entertainment. °By this means °we had been privileged to hear °Kipling's 'Mandalay', 'I'll Sing Thee Songs of Araby', 'The Midshipmite', and 'Ho, Jolly Jenkin!': and now the piano began to °tinkle again and a voice °broke into a less familiar °number.

The words came to us °faintly, but clearly:

'The days of °Chivalry are dead,
Of which in stories I have read,
When knights were °bold and acted °kind of °scrappy;
They used to °take a lot of pains
And fight all day to °please °the Janes,
And if their dame was tickled they was happy.
But now the men are mild and °meek:
They seem to °have a yellow streak:
They never °lay for other °guys, to °flatten 'em:
They think they've done a °darned fine thing
If they just buy the girl a ring
Of imitation diamonds and platinum.

'Oh, it makes me sort of sad
To think about °Sir Galahad

knightly ['naitli] *ritterlich*
quest [kwest] *Suche, Streben*
knightly quest *Ritterzug*
passage ['pæsidʒ] *Korridor, Gang*
bar-parlour ['bɑ:pɑ:lə] *Schankstube*
angler ['æŋglə] *Angler*
Stout and Mild ['staut ənd 'maild] *engl. Biersorten; die Gäste werden hier nach dem bezeichnet, was sie trinken*
the better *um so besser*
entertainment [entə'teinmənt] *Unterhaltung, hier: Darbietung*
by this means [bai ðis 'mi:nz] *dadurch*
we had been privileged ['privilidʒd] *wir hatten die Ehre gehabt*
Rudyard Kipling ['rʌdjəd 'kipliŋ] *engl. Schriftsteller, 1865–1936*
tinkle [tiŋkl] *hell klingen*
broke into ['brəuk 'intu] *von* break into *anstimmen*
number ['nʌmbə] *vorgetragene Nummer, Musikstück*
faintly ['feintli] *schwach*
chivalry ['ʃivəlri] *Ritterlichkeit; Rittertum*
bold [bəuld] *kühn*
kind of [kaind] *irgendwie*
scrappy *sl.* ['skræpi] *kampflustig*
take pains ['teik 'peinz] *sich die Mühe nehmen*
please [pli:z] *gefallen*
the Janes [dʒeinz] *hier: die Mädchen*
meek [mi:k] *sanft*
have a yellow streak [stri:k] *einen feigen Charakterzug haben*
lay for F [lei fɔ:] *auflauern*
guy [gai] *Kerl*
flatten ['flætn] *flach machen; hier: niederschlagen*

And all the knights of that romantic day:

To amuse a girl and °charm her
They would climb into their °armour
And jump into the °fray:
They called her "Lady love",
They used to wear her little glove,
And °everything that she said went:
For those were the days when a lady was a lady
And a °gent was a perfect gent.'

darned [dɑ:nd] *euphem. für* damned *verdammt*
sort of [sɔ:t] *irgendwie*
Sir Galahad [sə:ˈgæləhæd] *Ritter der Tafelrunde*

---

charm s.o. [tʃɑ:m] *j-n bezaubern*
armour [ˈɑ:mə] *Rüstung*
fray [frei] *Kampf*
everything that she said went *alles, was sie sagte, galt*
gent [dʒent] *Kurzform für* gentleman

A Ninepennyworth of Sherry sighed.

'True,' he murmured. 'Very true.'

The singer continued:

'Some night when they sat down to dine,
Sir Claude would say: "That girl of mine
Makes every woman °jealous when she sees her."
Then someone else would shout: °"Behave,
°Thou °malapert and °scurvy °knave,
Or I will °smite °thee one upon the °beezer!"
And then next morning in the °lists
They'd take their °lances in their fists
And mount a pair of °chargers, °highly mettled:
And when Sir Claude, so fair and young,
Got °punctured in the leg or lung,
They looked upon the °argument as settled.'

jealous [ˈdʒeləs] *eifersüchtig*

behave [biˈheiv] *sich benehmen*
thou [ðau] *du (veraltet)*
malapert [ˈmæləpə:t] *vermessen, unverschämt*
scurvy [ˈskə:vi] *räudig*
knave [neiv] *Schurke*
smite [smait] *humor. schlagen*
thee [ði:] *dich (veraltet)*
beezer *sl.* [ˈbi:zə] *„Gurke" (Nase)*
lists *Pl* [lists] *Turnierplatz*
lance [læns] *Lanze*
charger [ˈtʃɑ:dʒə] *Schlachtroß*
highly mettled [ˈhaili ˈmetld] *feurig*
got punctured [ˈpʌŋktʃəd] *von* get ... *durchbohrt werden*
settle an argument [ˈɑ:gjumənt] *einen Streit schlichten*

The Ninepennyworth of Sherry sighed again.

'He's right,' he said. 'We live in °degenerate days, gentlemen. Where

degenerate [diˈdʒenərit] *degeneriert*

now is the fine old tradition of °derring-do? Where,' demanded the Ninepenny-worth of Sherry with modest °fervour, 'shall we find in these °prosaic modern times the spirit that made the knights of old go through °perilous adventures and °brave dreadful dangers to do their lady's °behest?'

derring-do ['deriŋ'du:] *Verwegenheit*
fervour ['fə:və] *Eifer, Glut, Inbrunst*
prosaic [prəu'zeiik] *prosaisch*
perilous ['periləs] *gefährlich*
brave [breiv] *trotzen*
behest [bi'hest] *Geheiß, Befehl*

'In the Mulliner family,' said Mr. Mulliner, pausing for a moment from the °sipping of his hot Scotch and lemon, 'in the °clan to which I have the honour to belong, the spirit to which you °allude still °flourishes in all its °pristine °vigour. I can scarcely °exemplify this better than by relating the story of my cousin's son, Mervyn, and the strawberries.'

sip [sip] *schlürfen*
clan [klæn] *Sippe, Clan*
allude to [ə'lu:d] *anspielen auf*
flourish ['flʌriʃ] *blühen, gedeihen*
pristine ['pristain] *unverdorben*
vigour ['vigə] *Kraft*
exemplify [ig'zemplifai] *durch Beispiele erläutern*

'But I want to listen to the concert,' °pleaded a Rum and Milk. 'I just heard the °curate °clear his throat. That always means "Dangerous Dan McGrew".'

plead [pli:d] *flehentlich bitten*
curate ['kjuərit] *Hilfspfarrer*
clear one's throat ['kliə wʌnz 'θrəut] *sich räuspern*

'The story,' repeated Mr. Mulliner with °quiet °firmness, as he closed the door, 'of my cousin's son, Mervyn, and the strawberries.'

quiet ['kwaiət] *ruhig*
firmness ['fə:mnis] *Festigkeit, Unbeirrtheit*

In the circles in which the two moved (said Mr. Mulliner) it had often been °debated whether my cousin's son, Mervyn, was a bigger °chump than my nephew Archibald—the one who, if you recall, was so good at imitating a hen laying an egg. Some took one side, some the other; but, though the point still lies open, there is no °doubt that young Mervyn was quite a big enough chump for everyday use. And it was this quality in him that °deterred Clarice

debate [di'beit] *debattieren*
chump F [tʃʌmp] *Dummkopf, Trottel*
doubt [daut] *Zweifel*
deter [di'tə:] *abhalten*

Mallaby from °consenting to become his bride.

He discovered this one night when, as they were dancing at the Restless Cheese, he put the thing °squarely up to her, °not mincing his words.

'Tell me, Clarice,' he said, 'why is it that you °spurn a fellow's °suit? I can't for the life of me see why you won't consent to marry a °chap. It isn't as if I hadn't asked you often enough. °Playing fast and loose with a good man's love is the way I look at it.'

And he °gazed at her in a way that was partly melting and partly °suggestive of the °dominant male. And Clarice Mallaby gave one of those light, tinkling laughs and replied: 'Well, if you really want to know, you're such an ass.'

Mervyn could make nothing of this.

'An ass? How do you mean an ass? Do you mean a silly ass?'

'I mean a °goof,' said the girl. 'A °gump. A °poop. A °nitwit and a °returned °empty. Your name came up the other day in the course of conversation at home, and mother said you were a °vapid and °irreflective °guffin, totally °lacking in character and °purpose.'

'Oh?' said Mervyn. 'She did, did she?'

'She did. And while it isn't often that I °think along the same lines as mother, there—°for once—I consider her to have °hit the bull's-eye, °rung the bell, and to be entitled to a cigar or coco-nut, according to choice. It seemed to me what they call the °*mot juste*.'

'Indeed?' said Mervyn, °nettled. 'Well, let me tell you something. When it comes to °discussing brains, your

consent [kən'sent] *einwilligen*

squarely ['skwɛəli] *ohne Umschweife*

not to mince one's words [mins] *kein Blatt vor den Mund nehmen*

spurn [spə:n] *verschmähen*

suit [sju:t] *Antrag*

chap [tʃæp] *Bursche*

play fast and loose ['fɑ:st ənd 'lu:s] *Katz und Maus spielen*

gaze [geiz] *starren*

suggestive [sʌ'dʒestiv] *andeutend, erinnernd an*

dominant ['dɔminənt] *dominierend, überlegen*

goof [gu:f] *Tropf*

gump [gʌmp] *Schafskopf*

poop [pu:p] *Kurzform für* nincompoop *Einfaltspinsel*

nitwit ['nitwit] *Hohlkopf*

empty ['empti] *Leergut*

returned empty *hier: „Flasche"*

vapid ['væpid] *geistlos*

irreflective [iri'flektiv] *gedankenlos*

guffin *sl.* ['gʌfin] *Klotz*

s.o. is lacking in s.th. ['lækiŋ] *j-m fehlt es an et.*

purpose ['pə:pəs] *Entschlußkraft*

think along the same lines *gedanklich übereinstimmen*

for once *ausnahmsweise*

hit the bull's eye, ring the bell ['bulz ai, riŋ] *ins Schwarze treffen (Schießstand)*

mot juste [məu 'ʒust] *franz. richtiges Wort*

nettle ['netl] *ärgern, reizen*

discuss [dis'kʌs] *diskutieren, sprechen über*

mother, in my opinion, would do better to °recede modestly into the background and not try to set herself up as an authority. I strongly suspect her of being the woman who was seen in °Charing Cross Station the other day, asking a porter if he could direct her to Charing Cross Station. And, in the second place,' said Mervyn, 'I'll show you if I haven't got character and purpose. Set me some quest, like the knights of old, and see how quick I'll °deliver the goods as per °esteemed order.'

'How do you mean—a quest?'

'Why, °bid me do something for you, or get something for you, or °biff somebody in the eye for you. You know the °procedure.'

Clarice thought for a moment. Then she said: 'All my life I've wanted to eat strawberries in the middle of winter. Get me a basket of strawberries before the end of the month and we'll take up this °matrimonial proposition of yours in a spirit of serious °research.'

'Strawberries?' said Mervyn.

'Strawberries.'

Mervyn °gulped a little.

'Strawberries?'

'Strawberries.'

'But, I say, °dash it! *Strawberries?*'

'Strawberries,' said Clarice.

And then at last Mervyn, reading between the lines, saw that what she wanted was strawberries. And how he was to get any in December was more than he could have told you.

'I could do you oranges,' he said.

'Strawberries.'

'Or nuts. You wouldn't prefer a nice nut?'

recede [ri'siːd] *sich zurückziehen*

Charing Cross ['tʃɛəriŋ 'krɔs] *Platz im Zentrum Londons*

deliver [di'livə] *liefern*
esteemed [i'stiːmd] *geschätzt*
bid [bid] *heißen, befehlen*
biff *sl.* [bif] *hauen*
procedure [prə'siːdʒə] *Vorgang*

matrimonial proposition [mætri'məunjəl prɔpə'ziʃən] *Heiratsantrag*
research [ri'səːtʃ] *Forschung*

gulp [gʌlp] *schlucken, würgen*
dash it ['dæʃ it] *euphem. für damn it verdammt*

'Strawberries,' said the girl firmly. 'And you're jolly lucky, my lad, not to be sent off after the Holy °Grail or something, or told to °pluck me a °sprig of edelweiss from the top of the Alps. Mind you, I'm not saying yes and I'm not saying no, but this I will say—that if you bring me that basket of strawberries in the °stated time, I shall know that there's more in you than °sawdust—which °the casual observer wouldn't believe—and I will reopen your case and examine it thoroughly in the light of the fresh °evidence. Whereas, if you °fail to deliver the fruit, I shall know that mother was right, and you can jolly well make up your mind to °doing without my society from now on.'

Here she stopped to take in breath, and Mervyn, after a °lengthy pause, °braced himself up and managed to °utter a brave laugh. It was a little °roopy, if not actually °hacking, but he did it.

°'Right-ho,' he said. 'Right-ho. If that's the way you feel, well, °to put it in a nutshell, right-ho.'

My cousin's son Mervyn passed a restless night that night, °tossing on the °pillow not a little, and °feverishly at that. If this girl had been a °shade less attractive, he told himself, he would have sent her a telegram telling her to go to the °dickens. But, as it so happened, she was not; so the only thing that remained for him to do was to °pull up the old socks and °take a stab at the programme, as °outlined. And he was sipping his morning cup of tea, when something more or less °resembling an idea came to him.

Grail [greil] *Gral*
pluck [plʌk] *pflücken*
sprig [sprig] *Zweig*

stated ['steitid] *festgesetzt*
sawdust ['sɔːdʌst] *Sägespäne*
the casual observer ['kæʒjuəl əb'zəːvə] *der flüchtige Beobachter*
evidence ['evidəns] *Beweismaterial*
fail [feil] *versagen, nicht imstande sein*

do without *auskommen ohne*
lengthy pause ['leŋθi 'pɔːz] *längere Pause*
brace o.s. up [breis] *sich zusammenreißen*
utter ['ʌtə] *äußern, von sich geben*
roopy ['ruːpi] *heiser*
hacking ['hækiŋ] *stoßweise, stockend*
right-ho F ['rait'əu] *jawohl, in Ordnung*
to put it in a nutshell ['nʌtʃel] *um es kurz zu sagen*

toss [tɔs] *sich umherwerfen, sich wälzen*
pillow ['piləu] *Kopfkissen*
feverishly at that ['fiːvəriʃli] *fiebernd auch noch dazu*
shade [ʃeid] *Schattierung, hier:* F *Spur*
dickens ['dikinz] *euphem. für Teufel*
pull up the old socks *sl. sich in die Hände spucken*
take a stab at *sl.* [stæb] *es probieren mit*
outlined ['autlaind] *umrissen, skizziert*
resemble [ri'zembl] *ähnlich sehen*

He °reasoned thus. The wise man, finding himself in a dilemma, consults an expert. If, for example, some °knotty point of the law has °arisen, he will °proceed immediately in search of a legal expert, bring out his eight-and-six, and put the problem up to him. If it is a cross-word puzzle and he is stuck for the word in three letters, beginning with E and ending with U and meaning 'large Australian bird', he places the matter in the hands of the editor of the *Encyclopaedia Britannica*.

And, similarly, when the question confronting him is how to collect strawberries in December, the best plan is obviously to seek out that one of his °acquaintances who has the °most °established reputation for giving expensive parties.

This, Mervyn considered, was beyond a doubt Oofy Prosser. Thinking back, he could recall a dozen occasions when he had met °chorus-girls °groping their way along the street with a °dazed look in their eyes, and when he had asked them what the matter was they had explained that they were merely °living over again the exotic delights of the party Oofy Prosser had given last night. If anybody knew how to get strawberries in December, it would be Oofy.

He called, °accordingly, at the latter's apartment, and found him in bed, staring at the ceiling and °moaning in an undertone.

'Hullo!' said Mervyn. 'You look a bit red-eyed, old corpse.'

'I feel red-eyed,' said Oofy. 'And I wish, if it isn't absolutely necessary, that you wouldn't °come charging in

reason ['ri:zn] *hier: überlegen*
knotty ['nɔti] *verwickelt*
arisen [ə'rizn] *von* arise *auftreten*
proceed [prə'si:d] *sich anschicken*

acquaintance [ə'kweintəns] *Bekannte*
established [i'stæbliʃt] *feststehend, unzweifelhaft*
most established reputation [repju'teiʃən] *hier: unbestritten bester Ruf*
chorus-girl ['kɔ:rəs] *(Revue)-Tänzerin*
grope [grəup] *tasten*
dazed [deizd] *verwirrt, benebelt*
live over again *noch einmal durchleben*

accordingly [ə'kɔ:diŋli] *folglich*
moan [məun] *stöhnen*

come charging in ['tʃɑ:dʒiŋ] *hereinstürmen*

here early in the morning like this. By about ten o'clock to-night, I imagine, if I take great care of myself and keep quite quiet, I shall once more be in a position to look at °gargoyles without wincing; but at the moment the mere sight of your horrible face gives me an indefinable °shuddering feeling.'

'Did you have a party last night?'

'I did.'

'I wonder if by any chance you had strawberries?'

Oofy Prosser gave a sort of °quiver and shut his eyes. He seemed to be °wrestling with some powerful emotion. Then the °spasm passed, and he spoke.

'Don't talk about the beastly things,' he said. 'I never want to see strawberries again in my life. Nor °lobster, caviare, °pâté de foie gras, °prawns in aspic, or anything remotely resembling Bronx cocktails, Martinis, Side-Cars, Lizard's Breaths, All Quiet on the Western Fronts, and any variety of champagne, whisky, brandy, chartreuse, benedictine, and curaçao.'

Mervyn nodded sympathetically.

'I know just how you feel, old man,' he said. 'And I hate to have to °press the point. But I happen—for purposes which I will not °reveal—to require about a dozen strawberries.'

'Then go and buy them, °blast you,' said Oofy, turning his face to the wall.

'*Can* you buy strawberries in December?'

'Certainly. Bellamy's in °Piccadilly have them.'

'Are they frightfully expensive?' asked Mervyn, feeling in his pocket and fingering the one pound, two shillings

gargoyle ['gɑːgɔil] *Wasserspeier, hier: Scheusal*
shudder ['ʃʌdə] *erschaudern*

quiver ['kwivə] *(Er)Zittern*
wrestle ['resl] *ringen, kämpfen*
spasm ['spæzəm] *Krampf*

lobster ['lɔbstə] *Hummer*
pâté de foie gras ['pɑːtei də fwɑː'grɑː] *Gänseleberpastete*
prawn [prɔːn] *Garnele*

press the point *auf einem Punkt, einer Forderung bestehen*
reveal [ri'viːl] *enthüllen*
blast you [blɑːst] *hol dich der Kuckuck*

Piccadilly [pikə'dili] *Platz im Zentrum Londons*

and threepence which had got to last him to the end of the quarter when his °allowance came in. 'Do they cost a fearful lot?'

'Of course not. They're dirt cheap.'

Mervyn heaved a relieved sigh.

'I don't suppose I pay more than a pound apiece—or at most, thirty shillings—for mine,' said Oofy. 'You can get quite a lot for fifty °quid.'

Mervyn uttered a hollow groan.

'Don't °gargle,' said Oofy. 'Or, if you must gargle, gargle outside.'

'Fifty quid?' said Mervyn.

'Fifty or a hundred, I forget which. My man attends to these things.'

Mervyn looked at him in silence. He was trying to decide whether the moment had arrived to °put Oofy into circulation.

In the matter of borrowing money, my cousin's son, Mervyn, was °shrewd and °level-headed. He had °vision. At an early date he had come to the conclusion that it would be foolish to °fritter away a fellow like Oofy in a series of ten °bobs and quids. The prudent man, he felt, when he has an Oofy Prosser on his list, nurses him along till he feels the time is ripe for one of those quick Send-me-two-hundred-by-messenger-old-man-or-my-head-goes-in-the-gas-oven °touches. For years accordingly, he had been saving Oofy up for some really big °emergency.

And the point he had to decide was: Would there ever be a bigger emergency than this? That was what he asked himself.

Then it came home to him that Oofy was not in the mood. The way it

allowance [ə'lauəns] *Zuwendung, Taschengeld*

quid *sl.* [kwid] *Pfund Sterling*
gargle ['gɑːgl] *gurgeln*

put into circulation [səːkju'leiʃən] *in Umlauf setzen, zu Geld machen*
shrewd [ʃruːd] *schlau*
level-headed ['levl'hedid] *nüchtern, vernünftig*
vision ['viʒən] *Weitblick*

fritter away ['fritərə'wei] *vergeuden, verplempern*
bob *sl.* [bɔb] *engl. Schilling = 5 new pence*

touch *sl.* [tʌtʃ] *Anpumpen*
emergency [i'məːdʒənsi] *Notfall*

seemed to Mervyn was that, if Oofy's mother had crept to Oofy's bedside at this moment and tried to °mace him for as much as five bob, Oofy would have risen and struck her with the bromo-seltzer bottle.

With a soft sigh, therefore, he gave up the idea and °oozed out of the room and downstairs into Piccadilly.

Piccadilly looked pretty °mouldy to Mervyn. It was full, he tells me, of people and other foul things. He wandered along for a while in a °distrait way, and then suddenly out of the corner of his eye he became aware that he was in the presence of fruit. A shop on the °starboard side was full of it, and he discovered that he was standing outside Bellamy's.

And what is more, there, nestling in a basket in the middle of a lot of cotton-wool and blue paper, was a °platoon of strawberries.

And, as he gazed at them, Mervyn began to see how this thing could be worked with the minimum of discomfort and the maximum of profit °to all concerned. He had just remembered that his maternal uncle Joseph had an account at Bellamy's.

The next moment he had bounded through the door and was in conference with one of the °reduced °duchesses who do the fruit-selling at this particular °emporium. This one, Mervyn tells me, was about six feet high and looked down at him with large, °haughty eyes in a °derogatory manner—being, among other things, dressed °from stem to stern in black satin. He was conscious

mace s.o. for s.th. *sl.* [meis] *hier: j-n zwingen, et. herauszurücken, j-n um et. angehen*

ooze out ['u:z'aut] *entweichen*

mouldy ['məuldi] *schimmelig, muffig*

distrait [dis'trei] *zerstreut*

starboard side ['stɑ:bəd] *Steuerbordseite; rechte Seite*

platoon [plə'tu:n] *Gruppe, Aufgebot*

to all concerned [kən'sə:nd] *für alle Betroffenen*

reduced [ri'dju:st] *verarmt, heruntergekommen*
duchess ['dʌtʃis] *Herzogin*
emporium [em'pɔ:riəm] *Handelsplatz; Laden*
haughty ['hɔ:ti] *hochmütig*
derogatory [di'rɔgətəri] *herabsetzend*
from stem to stern ['stem tu 'stə:n] *von vorn bis achtern, hier: von Kopf bis Fuß*

of a slight chill, but he carried on according to plan.

'Good morning,' he said, switching on a smile and then switching it off again as he caught her eye. 'Do you sell fruit?'

If she had answered 'No', he would, of course, have been °nonplussed. But she did not. She inclined her head proudly.

°'Quate,' she said.

'That's fine,' said Mervyn heartily. 'Because fruit happens to be just what I'm after.'

'Quate.'

'I want that basket of strawberries in the window.'

'Quate.'

She reached for them and started to wrap them up. She did not seem to enjoy doing it. As she tied the string, her brooding look deepened. Mervyn thinks she may have had some great love-tragedy in her life.

'Send them to the Earl of Blotsam, 66A, Berkeley Square,' said Mervyn, alluding to his maternal uncle Joseph.

'Quate.'

'On second thoughts,' said Mervyn, 'no. I'll take them with me. Save trouble. Hand them over, and send the bill to Lord Blotsam.'

This, naturally, was the °crux or °nub of the whole °enterprise. And to Mervyn's concern, his suggestion did not seem to have met with the ready acceptance for which he had hoped. He had looked for the bright smile, the °courteous inclination of the head. Instead of which, the girl looked doubtful.

nonplussed ['nɔn'plʌst] *verwirrt, ratlos*

quate [kweit] *gewollt vornehme Aussprache für* quite, quite so *so ist es*

crux [krʌks] *lat. Kreuz; (der) wunde Punkt; Haken*

nub *AE* [nʌb] *(der) springende Punkt*

enterprise ['entəpraiz] *Unternehmen*

courteous ['kəːtjəs] *höflich*

'You °desi-ah to remove them in person?'

'Quate,' said Mervyn.

°'Podden me,' said the girl, suddenly disappearing.

She was not away long. In fact, Mervyn, °roaming °hither and thither about the shop, had barely had time to eat three or four dates and a °custard apple, when she was with him once more. And now she was wearing a look of definite °disapproval, like a duchess who has found half a °caterpillar in the castle salad.

'His lordship informs me that he desi-ahs no strawberries.'

'Eh?'

'I have been in telephonic communication with his lordship and he states °explicitly that he does not desi-ah strawberries.'

Mervyn °gave a little at the knees, but he came back stoutly.

'Don't you listen to what he says,' he °urged. °'He's always kidding. That's the sort of fellow he is. Just a great big happy schoolboy. Of course he desi-ahs strawberries. He told me so himself. I'm his nephew.'

°Good stuff, he felt, but it did not seem to be getting over. He caught a °glimpse of the girl's face, and it was definitely cold and hard and proud. However, he gave a careless laugh, just to show that his heart was in the right place, and seized the basket.

'Ha, ha!' he °tittered lightly, and started for the street at something midway between a °saunter and a gallop.

desi-ah [di'zaiɑː] *gewollt vornehme Aussprache für* desire
podden me ['pɔdn] *gewollt vornehme Aussprache für* pardon me

roam [rəum] *umherwandern*
hither and thither ['hiðər ənd 'ðiðə] *hierhin und dorthin*
custard apple ['kʌstəd] *Zimt-, Zuckerapfel*
disapproval [disə'pruːvəl] *Mißbilligung*
caterpillar ['kætəpilə] *Raupe*

explicitly [iks'plisitli] *ausdrücklich*

he gave a little at the knees [niːz] *ihm versagten die Knie ein wenig*
urge [əːdʒ] *drängen*
he is always kidding ['kidiŋ] *er neckt die Leute immer*

good stuff ['gud 'stʌf] *gutes Zeug, hier: das Richtige*
glimpse [glimps] *flüchtiger Blick*

titter ['titə] *kichern*

saunter ['sɔːntə] *Schlendern, Bummeln*

And he had not more than reached the open spaces when he heard the girl °give tongue behind him.

'EEEE — EEEE — EEEE — EEEE — EEEEEEEEEEE!' she said, °in substance.

Now, you must remember that all this took place round about the hour of noon, when every young fellow is at his lowest and weakest and the need for the °twelve-o'clock bracer has begun to °sap his °morale pretty considerably. With a couple of quick cold ones °under his °vest, Mervyn would, no doubt, have faced the situation and °carried it off with an air. He would have raised his eyebrows. He would have been °nonchalant and lit a °Murad. But, coming on him in his reduced condition, this fearful °screech unnerved him completely.

The duchess had now begun to cry 'Stop thief!' and Mervyn, most °injudiciously, instead of keeping his head and leaping carelessly into a passing taxi, made the grave °strategic error of picking up his feet with a jerk and starting to run along Piccadilly.

Well, naturally, that did him no good at all. Eight hundred people appeared from nowhere, willing hands gripped his collar and the seat of his trousers, and the next thing he knew he was cooling off in Vine Street Police Station.

After that, everything was more or less of a °blur. The scene seemed suddenly to change to a °police-court, in which he was confronted by a °magistrate who looked like an owl °with a dash of weasel blood in him.

give tongue [tʌŋ] *sich laut äußern*
in substance ['sʌbstəns] *hauptsächlich*

twelve o'clock bracer ['breisə] *Mittagstrunk*
sap [sæp] *untergraben, schwächen*
morale [mɔ'rɑ:l] *Moral, Kampfgeist*
vest [vest] *Unterhemd*
under his vest *hier: hinter der Binde*
carry it off with an air ['kæri, ɛə] *die Sache „stilvoll" (mit Anstand) durchstehen*
nonchalant ['nɔnʃələnt] *lässig, unbekümmert*
Murad ['mu:rəd] *Zigarettenmarke*
screech [skri:tʃ] *gellender Schrei*
injudiciously [indʒu'diʃəsli] *unklug*
strategic [strə'ti:dʒik] *strategisch*

blur [blə:] *hier: verwischter, nebelhafter Eindruck*
police-court [pə'li:s kɔ:t] *Polizeigericht*
magistrate ['mædʒistreit] *Polizeirichter; Friedensrichter*
with a dash of [dæʃ] *mit einem Spritzer*

A dialogue then took place, of which all he recalls is this:

POLICEMAN: °'Earing cries of 'Stop thief!' °your worship, and observing the accused running very °'earty, I °apprehended 'im.

MAGISTRATE: How did he appear, when apprehended?

POLICEMAN: Very °apprehensive, your worship.

MAGISTRATE: You mean he had a sort of °pinched look?

(*Laughter in court.*)

POLICEMAN: °It then transpired that 'e 'ad been attempting to °purloin strawberries.

MAGISTRATE: °He seems to have got the raspberry.

(*Laughter in court.*)

Well, what have you to say, young man?

MERVYN: Oh, ah!

MAGISTRATE: More °'owe' than 'ah', I fear.

(*Laughter in court, in which his worship joined.*)

Ten pounds or fourteen days.

Well, you can see how extremely unpleasant this must have been for my cousin's son. Considered purely from the dramatic °angle, the magistrate had °played him right off the stage, °hogging all the comedy and getting the sympathy of the audience from the start; and, apart from that, here he was, nearing the end of the quarter, with all his allowance spent except one pound, two and threepence, suddenly called upon to pay ten pounds or °go to durance vile for a matter of two weeks.

'Earing, 'earty, etc. ['iəriŋ, 'ɑːti] *im Cockney-Dialekt wird das h im Anlaut ausgelassen*
your worship ['wəːʃip] *Euer Ehren (Anrede bes. für hohe Amtspersonen)*
apprehend [æpri'hend] *ergreifen*
apprehensive [æpri'hensiv] *besorgt, ängstlich*
pinched [pinʃt] *bekümmert, bedrückt (Wortspiel mit* pinch F *klauen, stehlen)*
it transpired [træns'paiəd] *es „kam heraus"*
purloin [pəː'lɔin] *entwenden*
he seems to have got the raspberry ['rɑːzbəri] *er scheint eine Abfuhr bekommen zu haben*
owe [əu] *schulden (Wortspiel mit* oh*)*
angle ['æŋgl] *Winkel, hier: Standpunkt, Seite*
play s.o. off the stage [steidʒ] *j-n an die Wand spielen*
hog [hɔg] *an sich reißen*
go to durance vile ['djuərəns 'vail] *hinter Schloß und Riegel kommen*

There was only one course before him. His sensitive soul revolted at the thought of °languishing in a °dungeon for a solid fortnight, so it was °imperative that he raise the cash somewhere. And the only way of raising it that he could think of was to apply to his uncle, Lord Blotsam.

So he sent a messenger round to Berkeley Square, explaining that he was in jail and hoping his uncle was the same, and presently a letter was brought back by the butler, containing ten pounds in °postal orders, the Curse of the Blotsams, a third-class ticket to Blotsam Regis in Shropshire and instructions that, as soon as they °smote the °fetters from his wrists, he was to take the first train there and go and stay at Blotsam Castle till further notice.

Because at the castle, his uncle said in a powerful passage, even a blasted °pimply °pop-eyed good-for-nothing °scallywag and nincompoop like his nephew couldn't °get into mischief and disgrace the family name.

And in this, Mervyn tells me, there was a good deal of °rugged sense. Blotsam Castle, a noble °pile, is situated at least half a dozen miles from anywhere, and the only time anybody ever succeeded in disgracing the family name, while in residence, was back in the reign of °Edward the Confessor, when °the then Earl of Blotsam, having °lured a number of neighbouring landowners into the banqueting hall on the °specious °pretence of °standing them °mulled °sack, had proceeded to murder one and all with a battle-axe—°subsequently

languish ['læŋgwiʃ] *verschmachten*
dungeon ['dʌndʒən] *Verlies, Kerker*
imperative [im'perətiv] *unumgänglich*

postal order ['pəustəl 'ɔ:də] *Postanweisung*
smote [sməut] *von* smite, *hier: herunterschlagen*
fetters ['fetəz] *Fesseln*

pimply ['pimpli] *pickelig*
pop-eyed ['pɔpaid] *glotzäugig*
scallywag ['skæliwæg] *Lump*
get into mischief ['mistʃif] *etwas anstellen od. ausfressen*

rugged ['rʌgid] *rauh, hart*
pile [pail] *Gebäudekomplex*
Edward the Confessor ['edwəd ðə kən'fesə] *engl. König, 1042–1066*
the then *der damalige*
lure [ljuə] *locken*
specious ['spi:ʃəs] *bestechend, trügerisch, Schein ...*
pretence [pri'tens] *Vorwand*
stand [stænd] *hier: spendieren*
mull [mʌl] *(ein Getränk) heiß machen und (süß) würzen*

sack [sæk] *heller Süßwein*
subsequently ['sʌbsəkwentli] *anschließend*

cutting their heads off and—in rather loud taste—sticking them on spikes along the outer °battlements.

So Mervyn went down to Blotsam Regis and started to camp at the castle, and it was not long, he tells me, before he began to find the °time hanging a little heavy on his hands. For a couple of days he managed to endure the monotony, occupying himself in °carving the girl's initials on the immemorial elms with a heart round them. But on the third morning, having broken his Boy Scout pocket-knife, °he was at something of a loose end. And to fill in the time he started on a °moody stroll through the °messuages and °pleasances, feeling a good deal cast down.

After pacing hither and thither for a while, thinking of the girl Clarice, he came to a series of hothouses. And, it being extremely cold, with an east wind that went through his °plus-fours like a °javelin, he thought it would make an agreeable change if he were to go inside where it was warm and smoke two or perhaps three cigarettes.

And, scarcely had he got past the door, when he found he was almost entirely surrounded by strawberries. There they were, °scores of them, all °hot and juicy.

For a moment, he tells me, Mervyn had a sort of idea that a miracle had occurred. He seemed to remember a similar thing having happened to the Israelites in the desert—that time, he reminded me, when they were all saying to each other how well °a spot of manna would go down and what a dashed

battlements ['bætlmənts] *(Brustwehr mit) Zinnen*

time was hanging heavy on his hands *die Zeit wurde ihm lang*

carve [kɑːv] *schnitzen*

he was at a loose end [luːs end] *er wußte nicht, was er tun sollte*

moody ['muːdi] *trübsinnig, mißgestimmt*

messuage ['meswidʒ] *Wohnhaus mit Ländereien; Anwesen*

pleasance ['plezəns] *Lustgarten, Schloßpark*

plus-fours *Pl* ['plʌs'fɔːz] *weite Knickerbockerhose*

javelin ['dʒævlin] *Speer*

scores *Pl* [skɔːz] *Menge, große (An)Zahl*

hot [hɔt] *hier: ganz frisch*

a spot of [spɔt ɔv] *ein bißchen*

shame it was they hadn't any manna and that was the °slipshod way the commissariat department ran things and they wouldn't be surprised if it wasn't a case of °graft in high places, and then suddenly out of a blue sky all the manna °they could do with and enough over for breakfast next day.

slipshod ['slipʃɔd] *schlampig*

graft [grɑ:ft] *Korruption*

... they could do with ..., *das sie brauchen konnten*

Well, to be brief, that was the view which Mervyn took of the matter °in the first flush of his astonishment.

in the first flush [flʌʃ] *in der ersten Anwandlung*

Then he remembered that his uncle always opened the castle for the Christmas festivities, and these strawberries were, no doubt, intended for Exhibit A at some °forth-coming °rout or merry-making.

forthcoming ['fɔ:θkʌmiŋ] *bevorstehend*

rout [raut] *Abendgesellschaft*

Well, after that, of course, everything was simple. A child would have known what to do. Hastening back to the house, Mervyn returned with a °cardboard box and, °keeping a keen eye out for the head gardener, hurried in, selected about two dozen of the finest °specimens, placed them in the box, ran back to the house again, reached for the railway guide, found that there was a train leaving for London in an hour, changed into town clothes, seized his °top hat, borrowed the stable-boy's bicycle, °pedalled to the station, and about four hours later was mounting the front-door steps of Clarice Mallaby's house in Eaton Square with the box °tucked under his arm.

cardboard box ['kɑ:dbɔ:d-'bɔks] *Pappschachtel*

keeping a keen eye out for the head-gardener [ki:n, 'hed-gɑ:dnə] *wobei er scharf nach dem Obergärtner ausspähte*

specimen ['spesimin] *Exemplar*

top hat [tɔp hæt] *Zylinder (Hut)*

pedal ['pedl] *radeln*

tuck [tʌk] *stecken*

No, that is wrong. The box was not actually tucked under his arm, because he had left it in the train. Except for that, he had carried the thing through °without a hitch.

without a hitch [hitʃ] *reibungslos*

°Sturdy common sense is always a quality of the Mulliners, even of the less mentally gifted of the family. It was °obvious to Mervyn that no useful end was to be gained by ringing the bell and rushing into the girl's presence, shouting, 'See what I've brought you!'

On the other hand, what to do? He was feeling somewhat °unequal to the swirl of events.

Once, he tells me, some years ago, °he got involved in some amateur theatricals, to play the role of a butler: and his part consisted of the following lines and business:

(*Enter* JORKINS, *carrying telegram on* °*salver.*)

JORKINS: A telegram, m'lady.
(*Exit* JORKINS)

and on the night in he came, full of confidence, and, having said: 'A telegram, m'lady,' extended an empty salver towards the heroine, who, having been expecting on the strength of the telegram to °clutch at her heart and say: 'My God!' and °tear open the envelope and °crush it in nervous fingers and fall over in a °swoon, was considerably °taken aback, not to say °perturbed.

He felt now as he had felt then.

Still, he had enough sense left to see the way out. After a couple of turns up and down the south side of Eaton Square, he came—rather shrewdly, I must °confess—to the °conclusion that the only person who could help him in this emergency was Oofy Prosser.

The way Mervyn °sketched out the °scenario in the rough, °it all looked pretty plain sailing. He would go to

sturdy ['stə:di] *kräftig, robust, standhaft*
sturdy common sense ['kɔmən sens] *gesunder Menschenverstand*
obvious ['ɔbviəs] *offensichtlich*
unequal to the swirl of events ['ʌn'i:kwəl, swə:l, i'vents] *dem Trubel der Ereignisse nicht gewachsen*
he got involved [in'vɔlvd] *er wurde hineingezogen*
salver ['sælvə] *Tablett*
clutch at ['klʌtʃ ət] *(heftig) greifen nach*
tear [tɛə] *reißen*
crush [krʌʃ] *zerknüllen*
swoon [swu:n] *Ohnmacht*
taken aback ['teikən ə'bæk] *verblüfft*
perturbed [pə'tə:bd] *beunruhigt, verwirrt*
confess [kən'fes] *gestehen*
conclusion [kən'klu:ʒən] *Schluß(folgerung)*
sketch out ['sketʃ 'aut] *skizzieren, hier: sich ausmalen*
scenario [si'nɑ:riəu] *Drehbuch, hier: Szene*
... it looked pretty plain sailing ['plein 'seiliŋ] ..., *mußte alles ganz glatt gehen*

Oofy, whom, as I told you, he had been saving up for years, and with one single °impressive °gesture °get into his ribs for about twenty quid.

He would be losing money on the deal, of course, because he had always had Oofy °scheduled for at least fifty. But that could not be helped.

Then off to Bellamy's and buy strawberries. He did not exactly °relish the °prospect of meeting the black satin girl again, but when love is calling these things have to be done.

He found Oofy at home, and °plunged into the °agenda without °delay.

'Hullo, Oofy, old man!' he said. 'How are you, Oofy, old man? I say, Oofy, old man, I do like that tie you're wearing. What I call something like a tie. Quite the °snappiest thing I've seen for years and years and years and years. I wish I could get ties like that. But then, of course, I haven't your exquisite taste. What I've always said about you, Oofy, old man, and what I always will say, is that you have the most extraordinary °*flair*—it amounts to genius—in the selection of ties. But, then, one must °bear in mind that anything would look well on you, because you have such a clean-cut, °virile profile. I met a man the other day who said to me: "I didn't know °Ronald Colman was in England." And I said: "He isn't." And he said: "But I saw you talking to him outside the Blotto Kitten." And I said: "That wasn't Ronald Colman. That was my old °pal—the best pal any man ever had—Oofy Prosser." And he said: "Well, I never saw such a remarkable °resemblance." And I said: "Yes, there

impressive [im'presiv] *eindrucksvoll*
gesture ['dʒestʃə] *Geste*
get into his ribs for about twenty quid [ribz, kwid] *ihm ungefähr 20 Pfund abluchsen*
schedule ['ʃedju:l] *vorsehen, planen*

relish ['reliʃ] *genießen*
prospect ['prɔspekt] *Aussicht*
plunge [plʌndʒ] *sich stürzen*
agenda [ə'dʒendə] *Tagesordnung*
delay [di'lei] *Verzögerung*

snappy ['snæpi] *schick*

flair [flɛə] *Flair, Spürsinn*
bear in mind ['bɛərin'maind] *sich vor Augen halten*
virile ['virail] *männlich*
Ronald Colman ['rɔnəld 'kəulmən] *engl. Filmschauspieler*

pal F [pæl] *Kamerad, „Spezi", Freund*
resemblance [ri'zembləns] *Ähnlichkeit*

is a great resemblance, only, of course, Oofy is much the better-looking." And this fellow said: "Oofy Prosser? Is that *the* Oofy Prosser, the man whose name you hear everywhere?" And I said: "Yes, and I'm proud to call him my friend. I don't suppose," I said, "there's another fellow in London °in such demand. Duchesses °clamour for him, and, if you ask a princess to dinner, you have to add: 'To meet Oofy Prosser,' or she won't come. This," I explained, "is because, in addition to being the handsomest and best-dressed man in °Mayfair, he is famous for his °sparkling wit and °keen—but always kindly—repartee. And yet, in spite of all, he remains simple, unspoilt, unaffected." Will you lend me twenty quid, Oofy, old man?'

'No,' said Oofy Prosser.

Mervyn °paled.

'What did you say?'

'I said No.'

'No?'

'N—°ruddy—o!' said Oofy firmly.

Mervyn clutched at the mantelpiece.

'But, Oofy, old man, I need the money—need it °sorely.'

'I don't care.'

It seemed to Mervyn that the only thing to do was to tell all. Clearing his throat, he started in at the beginning. He sketched the course of his great love in burning words, and brought the story up to the point where the girl had placed her order for strawberries.

°'She must be cuckoo,' said Oofy Prosser.

Mervyn was respectful, but firm.

in such demand [di'mɑːnd] *so begehrt*
clamour for ['klæmə] *stürmisch verlangen nach*

Mayfair ['meifɛə] *elegantes Wohnviertel in London*
sparkling ['spɑːkliŋ] *sprühend*
keen repartee ['kiːn repɑː'tiː] *große Schlagfertigkeit*

pale [peil] *erblassen*

ruddy *sl.* ['rʌdi] *verflixt*
sorely ['sɔːli] *hier: dringend*

she must be cuckoo *sl.* ['kukuː] *sie muß spinnen*

'She isn't cuckoo,' he said. 'I have felt all along that the °incident showed what a °spiritual nature she has. I mean to say, reaching out yearningly for the °unattainable and all that sort of thing, if you know what I mean. Anyway, the broad, °basic point is that she wants strawberries, and I've got to collect enough money to get her them.'

incident ['insidənt] *Vorfall*
spiritual [spi'ritjuəl] *durchgeistigt*
unattainable ['ʌnə'teinəbl] *unerreichbar*
basic point ['beisik 'pɔint] *springender Punkt*

'Who is this °half-wit?' asked Oofy.

Mervyn told him, and Oofy seemed rather impressed.

'I know her.' He °mused awhile. 'Dashed pretty girl.'

half-wit ['hɑ:fwit] *Dummkopf*
muse [mju:z] *überlegen*

'Lovely,' said Mervyn. 'What eyes!'

'Yes.'

'What hair!'

'Yes.'

'What a figure!'

'Yes,' said Oofy. 'I always think she's one of the prettiest girls in London.'

'Absolutely,' said Mervyn. 'Then, on second thoughts, old pal, you will lend me twenty quid to buy her strawberries?'

'No,' said Oofy.

And Mervyn could not °shift him. In the end he gave it up.

shift [ʃift] *hier: dazu bewegen*

'Very well,' he said. 'Oh, very well. If you won't, you won't. But, Alexander Prosser,' proceeded Mervyn, with a good deal of °dignity, 'just let me tell you this. I wouldn't be seen dead in a tie like that °beastly thing you're wearing. I don't like your profile. Your hair is getting thin on the top. And I heard a certain prominent society hostess say the other day that the great drawback to living in London was that a woman couldn't give so much as the simplest luncheon-party without suddenly find-

dignity ['digniti] *Würde*
beastly ['bi:stli] *abscheulich*

ing that that °appalling man Prosser—I °quote her words—had °wriggled out of the woodwork and was in her midst. Prosser, I wish you a very good afternoon!'

Brave words, of course, but, when you came right down to it, they could not be said to have got him anywhere. After the first °thrill of telling Oofy what he thought of him had died away, Mervyn realized that his °quandary was now greater than ever. Where was he to look for °aid and °comfort? He had friends, of course, but the best of them wasn't good for more than an occasional drink or possibly a couple of quid, and what use was that to a man who needed at least a dozen strawberries at a pound apiece?

Extremely °bleak the world looked to my cousin's unfortunate son, and he was in °sombre mood as he wandered along Piccadilly. As he °surveyed the passing °populace, he suddenly realized, he tells me, °what these Bolshevist °blokes were driving at. They had °spotted—as he had spotted now—that what was wrong with the world was that all the °cash seemed to be centred in the wrong hands and needed a lot of °broad-minded °redistribution.

Where money was °concerned, he perceived, °merit counted for nothing. Money was too apt to be °collared by some °rotten °bounder or bounders, while the good and °deserving man was left standing on the outside, looking in. The sight of all those expensive cars rolling along, °crammed to the bulwarks with °overfed males and females

appalling [ə'pɔːliŋ] *entsetzlich*
quote [kwəut] *zitieren*
wriggle ['rigl] *sich winden wie ein Wurm*

thrill [θril] *Erregung, Spannung*
quandary ['kwɔndəri] *Dilemma*
aid [eid] *Hilfe*
comfort ['kʌmfət] *Trost*

bleak [bliːk] *trostlos, trübe*
sombre ['sɔmbə] *düster*
survey [səː'vei] *betrachten*
populace ['pɔpjuləs] *Massen, Pöbel*
bloke [bləuk] *Kerl, Bursche*
what they were driving at *worauf sie hinauswollten*
spot [spɔt] *herausfinden*

cash [kæʃ] *Geld*
broad-minded ['brɔːdmaindid] *großzügig*
redistribution ['riːdistri'bjuːʃən] *Neuverteilung*
concern [kən'səːn] *betreffen*
merit ['merit] *Verdienst*
collar F ['kɔlə] *schnappen, an sich reißen*
rotten ['rɔtn] *elend*
bounder *sl.* ['baundə] *Schurke*
deserving [di'zəːviŋ] *verdienstvoll, verdient*
crammed to the bulwarks [kræmd, 'bulwəks] *hier: vollgestopft bis zum Rande*
overfed ['əuvə'fed] *überfüttert*

with fur-coats and double chins, made him feel, he tells me, that he wanted to buy a red tie and a couple of bombs and start the Social Revolution. If Stalin had come along at that moment, Mervyn would have shaken him by the hand.

Well, there is, of course, only one thing for a young man to do when he feels like that. Mervyn hurried along to the club and in rapid succession drank three Martini cocktails.

The treatment was °effective, as it always is. °Gradually the °stern, °censorious mood passed, and he began to feel an optimistic glow. As the °revivers °slid over the °larynx, he saw that all was not lost. He perceived that he had been leaving out of his reckoning that sweet, °angelic pity which is such a characteristic of woman.

Take the case of a knight of old, he meant to say. Was anyone going to tell him that if a knight of old had been sent off by a °damsel on some fearfully °tricky quest and had gone through all sorts of °perils and °privations for her sake, facing dragons in black satin and risking going to °choky and what not, the girl would have °given him the bird when he got back, simply because—looking at the matter from a severely technical standpoint—he had failed to bring home the °gravy?

Absolutely not, Mervyn considered. She would have °been most awfully braced with him for °putting up such a good show and would have comforted and °cosseted him.

This girl Clarice, he felt, °was bound to do the same, so obviously the °move now was to °toddle along to Eaton

effective [i'fektiv] *wirksam*
gradually ['grædjuəli] *allmählich*
stern [stə:n] *streng*
censorious [sen'sɔ:riəs] *kritisch, tadelsüchtig*
reviver [ri'vaivə] *Wiederbelebungsmittel*
slid [slid] *von* slide *gleiten, rutschen*
larynx ['læriŋks] *Kehle*
angelic [æn'dʒelik] *engelgleich*

damsel ['dæmzəl] *Maid*
tricky ['triki] *riskant*
peril ['peril] *Gefahr*
privation [prai'veiʃən] *Entbehrung*
choky *sl.* ['tʃəuki] Kittchen
give s.o. the bird *j-n abweisen*

gravy *sl.* ['greivi] *(unverhoffter) Gewinn*
be braced with [breist] *hier: verbunden sein od. erfreut sein mit*
put up a good show *etwa: sich tapfer schlagen*
cosset ['kɔsit] *verhätscheln*
be bound to do [baund] *tun müssen*
move [mu:v] *hier: (der nächste) Schritt*
toddle ['tɔdl] *dahinzotteln; abhauen*

Square again and explain matters to her. So he gave his hat a brush, °flicked a spot of dust from his coat-sleeve, and shot off in a taxi.

All during the drive he was °rehearsing what he would say to her, and it sounded pretty good to him. In his mind's eye he could see the tears coming into her gentle eyes as he told her about the Arm of the Law °gripping his trouser-seat. But, when he arrived, a hitch occurred. There was a °stage wait. The butler at Eaton Square told him the girl was dressing.

'Say that Mr. Mulliner has called,' said Mervyn.

So the butler went upstairs, and presently from aloft there came the clear °penetrating voice of his loved one telling the butler to °bung Mr. Mulliner into the °drawing-room and °lock up all the silver.

And Mervyn went into the drawing-room and settled down to wait.

It was one of those drawing-rooms where there is not a great deal to entertain and amuse the visitor. Mervyn tells me that he got a good laugh out of a photograph of the girl's °late father on the mantelpiece—a heavily-whiskered old gentleman who reminded him of a °burst horse-hair sofa—but the rest of the °appointments were on the dull side. They consisted of an album of views of Italy and a copy of Indian Love Lyrics bound in °limp cloth: and it was not long before he began to feel a touch of °ennui.

He polished his shoes with one of the sofa-cushions, and took his hat from the table where he had placed it and

flick [flik] *(weg)schnippen*
rehearse [ri'hɜːs] *proben*
grip [grip] *ergreifen, packen*
stage wait ['steidʒ'weit] *dramatische Pause*
penetrating ['penitreitiŋ] *durchdringend*
bung *sl.* [bʌŋ] *schleudern, schmeißen*
drawing-room ['drɔiŋrum] *Salon*
lock up ['lɔk'ʌp] *ver-, einsperren*
late [leit] *verstorben*
burst [bɜːst] *bersten, platzen*
appointments *Pl* [ə'pɔintmənts] *hier: Einrichtung, Ausstattung*
limp [limp] *weich, biegsam*
ennui [ɑ̃ː'nwiː] *franz. Langeweile*

gave it another brush: but after that there seemed to be nothing in the way of intellectual occupation offering itself, so he just leaned back in a chair and °unhinged his °lower jaw and let it °droop, and sank into a sort of °coma. And it was while he was still in this trance that he was delighted to hear a dog-fight in progress in the street. He went to the window and looked out, but the thing was °apparently taking place somewhere near the front door, and the top of the °porch hid it from him.

Now, Mervyn hated to miss a dog-fight. Many of his happiest hours had been spent at dog-fights. And this one appeared from the sound of it to be °on a more or less major scale. He ran down the stairs and opened the front door.

As his trained senses had told him, °the encounter was being staged at the foot of the steps. He stood in the open doorway and drank it in. He had always °maintained that you got the best dog-fights down in the Eaton Square neighbourhood, because there tough animals from the King's Road, Chelsea, district, were apt to wander in—dogs °who had trained on gin and flat-irons at the local public-houses and could be relied on to give of their best.

The present encounter °bore out this view. It was between a sort of °*consommé* of °mastiff and Irish terrier, on the one hand, and, on the other, a long-haired °*macédoine* of about seven °breeds of dog who had an °indescribable °raffish look, as if he had been mixing with the artist colony down by the river. For about five minutes it was

unhinge ['ʌn'hindʒ] *aus den Angeln heben; ausrenken*
lower jaw ['ləuə'dʒɔː] *Unterkiefer*
droop [druːp] *schlaff herabhängen*
coma ['kəumə] *Dämmerzustand*
apparently [ə'pærəntli] *anscheinend*
porch [pɔːtʃ] *Vorbau*
on a major scale ['meidʒə 'skeil] *in größerem Maßstab*
the encounter was being staged [in'kauntə] *die Begegnung fand statt*
maintain [mein'tein] *eine Meinung verfechten*
who had trained on gin and flat-irons [dʒin, 'flæt'aiənz] *die an Schnaps und (nachgeworfene) Bügeleisen gewöhnt waren*
bore out [bɔː] *von* bear out *bestätigen*
consommé [kən'sɔmei] *hier: das Produkt (einer Vereinigung zwischen...)*
mastiff ['mæstif] *Bulldogge*
macédoine [mæsə'dwɑːn] *Mischung, hier: Mischmasch, Durcheinander, „Promenadenmischung"*
breed [briːd] *Rasse*
indescribably ['indis'kraibəbli] *unbeschreiblich*
raffish ['ræfiʃ] *ordinär*

as inspiring a contest as you could have wished to see; but at the end of that time it stopped suddenly, both principals °simultaneously observing a cat at an °area gate down the road and °shaking hands hastily and °woofing after her.

Mervyn was not a little disappointed at this abrupt conclusion to the entertainment, but it was no use °repining. He started to go back into the house and was just closing the front door, when a °messenger-boy appeared, carrying a parcel.

'Sign, please,' said the messenger-boy.

The lad's mistake was a natural one. Finding Mervyn standing in the doorway without a hat, he had °assumed him to be the butler. He pushed the parcel into his hand, made him sign a yellow paper, and went off, leaving Mervyn with the parcel.

And Mervyn, glancing at it, saw that it was addressed to the girl–Clarice.

But it was not this that made him °reel where he stood. What made him reel where he stood was the fact that on the paper outside the thing was a label with 'Bellamy & Co., °Bespoke Fruitists' on it. And he was convinced, °prodding it, that there was some °squashy substance inside which certainly was not apples, oranges, nuts, bananas, or anything of that nature.

Mervyn lowered his °shapely nose and gave a good hard °sniff at the parcel. And, having done so, he reeled where he stood once more.

A frightful suspicion had shot through him.

simultaneously [siməl'teinjəsli] *gleichzeitig*
area ['ɛəriə] *hier: Kellervorhof*
shaking hands ['ʃeikiŋ 'hændz] *mit sportlichen Kämpfern verglichen*
woofing ['wu:fiŋ] *kläffend*
repine [ri'pain] *murren*

messenger-boy ['mesindʒəbɔi] *Botenjunge, Laufbursche*

assume [ə'sju:m] *annehmen*

reel [ri:l] *taumeln*

bespoke [bi'spəuk] *individuelle Aufträge erfüllend*
prod [prɔd] *hineinstechen, hineinbohren*
squashy ['skwɔʃi] *weich, matschig*

shapely ['ʃeipli] *wohlgeformt*
sniff [snif] *Schnüffeln*

It was not that my cousin's son was gifted beyond the ordinary in the qualities that go to make a successful detective. You would not have found him °deducing anything much from footprints or cigar-ash. In fact, if this parcel had contained cigar-ash, it would have meant nothing to him. But in the circumstances anybody with his special knowledge would have been suspicious.

For consider the facts. His sniff had told him that beneath the outward wrapping of paper lay strawberries. And the only person beside himself who knew that the girl wanted strawberries was Oofy Prosser. About the only man in London able to buy strawberries at that time of year was Oofy. And Oofy's manner, he °recalled, when they were talking about the girl's beauty and °physique generally, had been °furtive and °sinister.

To rip open the paper, therefore, and take a look at the enclosed card was with Mervyn Mulliner the work of a moment.

And, sure enough, it was as he had foreseen. 'Alexander C. Prosser' was the name on the card, and Mervyn tells me he wouldn't be a bit surprised if the C. didn't stand for 'Clarence'.

His first feeling, he tells me, as he stood there staring at that card, was one of °righteous indignation at the thought that any such °treacherous, °double-crossing hound as Oofy Prosser should have been permitted to °pollute the air of London, W.1, all these years. To °refuse a fellow twenty quid with one hand, and then to go and send his girl strawberries with the other, struck

deduce [di'dju:s] *ableiten, folgern*

recall [ri'kɔ:l] *sich ins Gedächtnis zurückrufen*
physique [fi'zi:k] *Körper(bau)*
furtive ['fə:tiv] *hinterhältig*
sinister ['sinistə] *unheilvoll*

righteous indignation ['raitʃəs indig'neiʃən] *gerechtfertigter Unwillen, gerechter Zorn*
treacherous ['tretʃərəs] *verräterisch*
double-crossing ['dʌbl'krɔsiŋ] *betrügerisch*
pollute [pə'lu:t] *verunreinigen*
refuse [ri'fju:z] *verweigern*

Mervyn as about as °low-down a bit of °hornswoggling as you could want.

He burned with honest wrath. And he was still burning when the last cocktail he had had at the club, which had been lying low inside him all this while, suddenly came to life and got action. Quite unexpectedly, he tells me, it began to °frisk about like a young lamb, until it leaped into his head and gave him the idea of a lifetime.

What, he asked himself, was the matter with °suppressing this card, °freezing on to the berries, and °presenting them to the girl with a modest flourish as coming from M. Mulliner, Esq.? And, he answered himself, there was °abso-°bally-nothing the matter with it. It was a jolly sound scheme and showed what three medium dry Martinis could do.

He quivered all over with joy and °elation. Standing there in the hall, he felt that there was a °Providence, after all, which kept an eye on good men and saw to it that they came out on top in the end. In fact, he felt so extremely °elated that he burst into song. And he had not got much beyond the first high note when he heard Clarice Mallaby giving tongue from upstairs.

'Stop it!'

'What did you say?' said Mervyn.

'I said "Stop it!" The cat's downstairs with a headache, trying to rest.'

'I say,' said Mervyn, 'are you going to be long?'

'How do you mean—long?'

'Long dressing. Because I've something I want to show you.'

'What?'

low-down ['ləudaun] *niederträchtig, gemein*

hornswoggling *sl.* ['hɔːnswɔgliŋ] *Hintergeherei, Betrügerei*

frisk [frisk] *hüpfen*

suppress [sə'pres] *verheimlichen, unterschlagen*

freeze on to [friːz] *sich krampfhaft festhalten an, hier: an sich nehmen, behalten*

present with a flourish [pri'zent, 'flʌriʃ] *hier: schwungvoll überreichen*

bally *sl.* ['bæli] *verflixt, verdammt*

abso-bally-nothing = absolutely nothing, *etwa: da ist doch zum Teufel nichts dagegen einzuwenden*

elation [i'leiʃən] *gehobene Stimmung*

Providence ['prɔvidəns] *Vorsehung*

elated [i'leitid] *in gehobener Stimmung*

'Oh, nothing much,' said Mervyn carelessly. 'Nothing particular. Just a few °assorted strawberries.'

'Eek!' said the girl. 'You don't mean you've really got them?'

'Got them?' said Mervyn. 'Didn't I say I would?'

'I'll be down in just one minute,' said the girl.

Well, you know what girls are. The minute stretched into five minutes, and the five minutes into a quarter of an hour, and Mervyn made the tour of the drawing-room, and looked at the photograph of her late father, and picked up the album of Views of Italy, and opened Indian Love Lyrics at page forty-three and shut it again, and took up the cushion and gave his shoes another rub, and brushed his hat once more, and still she didn't come.

And so, by way of something else to do, he started °brooding on the strawberries °for a space.

Considered purely as strawberries, he tells me, they were a pretty °rickety collection, not to say °spavined. They were an unhealthy whitish-pink in colour and looked as if they had just come through a lingering illness which had involved a good deal of blood-letting by means of leeches.

'They don't look much,' said Mervyn to himself.

Not that it really mattered, of course, because all the girl had told him to do was to get her strawberries, and nobody could deny that these were strawberries. °C.3 though they might be, they were genuine strawberries, and from that fact there was no getting away.

assorted [ə'sɔːtid] *hier: ausgesucht*

brood on ['bruːd ɔn] *brüten od. grübeln über*

for a space [speis] *hier: eine Zeitlang*

rickety ['rikiti] *schäbig*

spavin ['spævin] *Spat, eine Pferdekrankheit*

not to say spavined ['spævind] *etwa: um nicht zu sagen, krank aussehend*

C. 3 *schlechte Qualität (Gegensatz: A 1)*

Still, he did not want the dear little soul to be disappointed.

'I wonder if they have any °flavour at all?' said Mervyn to himself.

Well, the first one had not. Nor had the second. The third was rather better. And the fourth was quite juicy. And the best of all, oddly enough, was the last one in the basket.

He was just finishing it when Clarice Mallaby came running in.

Well, Mervyn °tried to pass it off, of course. But his °efforts were not rewarded with any great measure of success. In fact, he tells me that he did not get beyond a °tentative 'Oh, I say ...' And the °upshot of the whole matter was that the girl threw him out into the winter evening without so much as giving him a chance to take his hat.

Nor had he the courage to go back and fetch it later, for Clarice Mallaby stated °specifically that if he dared to show his ugly face at the house again the butler had instructions to knock him down and °skin him, and the butler was looking forward to it, as he had never liked Mervyn.

So there the matter rests. The whole thing has been a great blow to my cousin's son, for he considers—and rightly, I suppose—that, if you really come down to it, he failed in his quest. Nevertheless, I think that we must °give him credit for the possession of the old knightly spirit to which our friend here was alluding just now.

He meant well. He did his best. And even of a Mulliner more cannot be said than that.

flavour ['fleivə] *Aroma*

he tried to pass it off *er versuchte sich 'rauszureden*
effort ['efət] *Anstrengung, Bemühung*
tentative ['tentətiv] *zaghaft, zögernd*
upshot ['ʌpʃɔt] *Ergebnis, Ausgang*

specifically [spi'sifikəli] *mit Bestimmtheit, Nachdruck*
skin [skin] *die Haut abziehen*

give s.o. credit for s.th. ['kredit] *j-m et. hoch anrechnen*

My Oedipus Complex

BY FRANK O'CONNOR

FATHER was in the army all through the war—the First War, I mean—so, up to the age of five, I never saw much of him, and what I saw did not worry me. Sometimes I woke and there was a big figure in khaki peering down at me in the candlelight. Sometimes in the early morning I heard the °slamming of the front door and the °clatter of nailed boots down the °cobbles of the lane. These were Father's °entrances and exits. Like Santa Claus he came and went mysteriously.

In fact, I rather liked his visits, though it was an uncomfortable °squeeze between Mother and him when I got into the big bed in the early morning. He smoked, which gave him a pleasant °musty smell, and shaved, an operation of °astounding interest. Each time he left a °trail of souvenirs—model tanks and °Gurkha knives with handles made of °bullet cases, and German helmets and cap °badges and °button-sticks, and all sorts of military equipment—carefully °stowed away in a long box on top of the wardrobe, in case they ever °came in handy. There was a bit of the °magpie about Father; he expected everything to come in handy. When his back was turned, Mother let me get a chair and °rummage through his treasures. She didn't seem to think so highly of them as he did.

The war was the most peaceful period of my life. The window of my °attic

slamming ['slæmiŋ] *Zuschlagen*
clatter ['klætə] *Klappern*
cobble ['kɔbl] *Pflasterstein*
entrances and exits ['entrənsiz, 'eksits] *hier: Kommen und Gehen*
squeeze [skwi:z] *Zusammendrängen*
musty ['mʌsti] *muffig*
astounding [ə'staundiŋ] *erstaunlich*
trail [treil] *Spur*
Gurkha ['gə:kə] *Gurkha, Mitglied eines indischen Stammes in Nepal*
bullet case ['bulit keis] *Gewehrpatronenhülse*
badge [bædʒ] *Abzeichen*
button-stick ['bʌtn stik] *milit. Knopfgabel*
stow away [stəu ə'wei] *verstauen*
came in handy ['hændi] *von come... gut zu gebrauchen sein*
magpie ['mægpai] *Elster*
rummage ['rʌmidʒ] *wühlen*
attic ['ætik] *Mansarde*

faced south-east. My Mother had curtained it, but that had small effect. I always woke with the first light and, with all the °responsibilities of the °previous day melted, feeling myself rather like the sun, ready to illumine and °rejoice. Life never seemed so simple and clear and full of possibilities as then. I put my feet out from under the clothes—I called them Mrs Left and Mrs Right—and invented dramatic situations for them in which they discussed the problems of the day. At least Mrs Right did; she was very °demonstrative, but I hadn't the same control of Mrs Left, so °she mostly contented herself with nodding agreement.

They discussed what Mother and I should do during the day, what Santa Claus should give a fellow for Christmas, and what steps should be taken to brighten the home. There was that little matter of the baby, for instance. Mother and I could never agree about that. Ours was the only house in the °terrace without a new baby, and Mother said we °couldn't afford one till Father came back from the war because they cost °seventeen and six. That showed how simple she was. The Geneys up the road had a baby, and everyone knew they couldn't afford seventeen and six. It was probably a cheap baby, and Mother wanted something really good, but I felt she was too exclusive. °The Geneys' baby would have done us fine.

Having settled my plans for the day, I got up, put a chair under the attic window, and °lifted the frame high enough to stick out my head. The win-

responsibility [rispɔnsə'biliti] *Verantwortlichkeit, Verpflichtung*
previous ['pri:vjəs] *vorhergehend*
rejoice [ri'dʒɔis] *frohlocken*

demonstrative [di'mɔnstrətiv] *hinweisend, hier: überschwenglich*
she contented herself [kən'tentid] *sie gab sich zufrieden*

terrace ['terəs] *Häuserreihe ursprünglich an erhöht gelegener Straße*
could afford [ə'fɔ:d] *von* can … *sich leisten können*
seventeen and six *17 shillings and 6 pence; damals hatte ein £ 20 shillings und ein shilling 12 pence, während jetzt ein £ hundert pence hat. Der Betrag entspricht jetzt 87½ pence.*

the Geney's baby would have done us fine F *das Baby der G. wäre für uns gut genug gewesen*
lift the frame [freim] *den Rahmen (des Schiebefensters) hochschieben*

dow overlooked the front gardens of the terrace behind ours, and beyond these it looked over a deep valley to the tall, red-brick houses terraced up the opposite hillside, which were all still in shadow, while those at our side of the valley were all lit up, though with long strange shadows that made them seem °unfamiliar; °rigid and painted.

After that I went into Mother's room and climbed into the big bed. She woke and I began to tell her of my °schemes. By this time, though I never seem to have noticed it, I was °petrified in my nightshirt, and I thawed as I talked until, the last frost melted, I fell asleep beside her and woke again only when I heard her below in the kitchen, making the breakfast.

After breakfast we went into town; heard Mass at St Augustine's and said a prayer for Father, and did the shopping. If the afternoon was fine we either went for a walk in the country or a visit to Mother's great friend in the convent, Mother St Dominic. °Mother had them all praying for Father, and every night, going to bed, I asked God to send him back safe from the war to us. Little, indeed, did I know what I was praying for!

One morning I got into the big bed, and there, sure enough, was Father in his usual Santa Claus manner, but later, instead of uniform, he put on his best blue suit, and Mother was as pleased as anything. I saw nothing to be pleased about, because, out of uniform, Father was altogether less interesting, but she only °beamed, and explained that our prayers had been answered, and off we

unfamiliar ['ʌnfə'miljə] *nicht vertraut*
rigid ['ridʒid] *streng, steif*

scheme [skiːm] *Plan*
petrified ['petrifaid] *zu Stein erstarrt*

mother had them all praying ['preiiŋ] *Mutter ließ sie alle beten*

beam [biːm] *strahlen, glücklich aussehen*

went to Mass to thank God for having brought Father safely home.

The irony of it! That very day when he came in to dinner he took off his boots and put on his slippers, °donned the dirty old cap he wore about the house to save him from colds, crossed his legs, and began to talk °gravely to Mother, who looked °anxious. Naturally, I disliked her looking anxious, because it °destroyed her good looks, so I °interrupted him.

'Just a moment, Larry!' she said gently.

This was only what she said when we had °boring visitors, so I attached no importance to it and went on talking.

'Do be quiet, Larry!' she said °impatiently. 'Don't you hear me talking to Daddy?'

This was the first time I had heard those °ominous words, 'talking to Daddy', and I couldn't help feeling that if this was how God answered prayers, he couldn't listen to them very attentively.

'Why are you talking to Daddy?' I asked with as great a show of indifference as I could °muster.

'Because Daddy and I have business to discuss. Now don't interrupt again!'

In the afternoon, at Mother's °request, Father took me for a walk. This time we went into town instead of out to the country, and I thought at first, in my usual optimistic way, that it might be an °improvement. It was nothing of the sort. Father and I had quite different °notions of a walk in town. He had no proper interest in trams, ships, and horses, and the only thing that seemed

don [dɔn] *aufsetzen, anziehen*

gravely ['greivli] *ernst*
anxious ['æŋkʃəs] *besorgt*
destroy [di'strɔi] *zerstören*
interrupt [intə'rʌpt] *unterbrechen*

boring ['bɔːriŋ] *langweilig*
impatiently [im'peiʃəntli] *ungeduldig*

ominous ['ɔminəs] *unheilvoll*

muster ['mʌstə] *aufbringen*
request [ri'kwest] *Bitte, Ersuchen*

improvement [im'pruːvmənt] *Verbesserung*
notion ['nəuʃən] *Begriff, Vorstellung*

to °divert him was talking to fellows as old as himself. When I wanted to stop he simply went on, dragging me behind him by the hand; when he wanted to stop °I had no alternative but to do the same. I noticed that it seemed to be a sign that he wanted to stop for a long time whenever he leaned against a wall. The second time I saw him do it I got wild. He seemed to be settling himself forever. I pulled him by the coat and trousers, but, unlike Mother who, if you were too °persistent, °got into a wax and said: 'Larry, if you don't behave yourself, I'll give you a good °slap,' Father had an extraordinary °capacity for °amiable inattention. °I sized him up and wondered would I cry, but he seemed to be too °remote to be annoyed even by that. Really, it was like going for a walk with a mountain! He either ignored °the wrenching and pummelling entirely, or else glanced down with a grin of amusement from his °peak. I had never met anyone so °absorbed in himself as he seemed.

At teatime, 'talking to Daddy' began again, complicated this time by the fact that he had an evening paper, and every few minutes he put it down and told Mother something new out of it. I felt this was foul play. Man for man, I was prepared to °compete with him any time for Mother's attention, but when he had it all made up for him by other people it left me no chance. Several times I tried to change the subject without success.

'You must be quiet while Daddy is reading, Larry,' Mother said impatiently.

divert [dai'vəːt] *zerstreuen, unterhalten*

I had no alternative [ɔːl'təːnətiv] *ich hatte keine andere Wahl*

persistent [pə'sistənt] *beharrlich, hartnäckig*

she got into a wax *sl.* [wæks] *sie bekam eine Stinkwut*

slap [slæp] *Schlag, Klaps*

capacity [kə'pæsiti] *(Leistungs)Fähigkeit*

amiable ['eimjəbl] *liebenswürdig, freundlich*

I sized him up [saizd] *ich schätzte ihn ein, beurteilte ihn*

remote [ri'məut] *(weit) entfernt*

the wrenching and pummelling ['renʃiŋ, 'pʌməliŋ] *das Zerren und mit den Fäusten Schlagen*

peak [piːk] *Gipfel, Höhe*

absorbed [əb'sɔːbd] *versunken, vertieft*

compete [kəm'piːt] *sich messen*

It was clear that she either °genuinely liked talking to Father better than talking to me, or else that he °had some terrible hold on her which made her afraid to admit the truth.

'Mummy,' I said that night when she was °tucking me up, 'do you think if I prayed hard God would send Daddy back to the war?'

She seemed to think about that for a moment.

'No, dear,' she said with a smile. 'I don't think he would.'

'Why wouldn't he, Mummy?'

'Because there isn't a war any longer, dear.'

'But, Mummy, couldn't God make another war, if He liked?'

'He wouldn't like to, dear. It's not God who makes wars, but bad people.'

'Oh!' I said.

I was disappointed about that. I began to think that °God wasn't quite what he was cracked up to be.

Next morning I woke at my usual hour, feeling like a bottle of champagne. I put out my feet and invented a long conversation in which Mrs Right talked of the trouble she had with her own father till she put him in the Home. I didn't quite know what the Home was but it sounded the right place for Father. Then I got my chair and stuck my head out of the attic window. °Dawn was just breaking, with a °guilty air that made me feel I had °caught it in the act. My head bursting with stories and schemes, I °stumbled in next door, and in the half-darkness °scrambled into the big bed. There was no room at Mother's side so I had to get between her and Father.

genuinely ['dʒenjuinli] *echt, wirklich*
have a hold on [həuld] *Macht haben über*

tuck up [tʌk 'ʌp] *ins Bett stekken*

God wasn't quite what he was cracked up to be *sl.* [krækt] *Gott war doch nicht ganz so, wie man uns glauben machen wollte*

dawn [dɔ:n] *Morgendämmerung*
guilty air ['gilti 'ɛə] *schuldbewußte Miene*
caught in the act [kɔ:t, ækt] *auf frischer Tat ertappt*
stumble ['stʌmbl] *purzeln, stolpern*
scramble ['skræmbl] *krabbeln, klettern*

For the time being I had forgotten about him, and for several minutes I sat °bolt upright, °racking my brains to know what I could do with him. He was taking up more than his fair share of the bed, and I couldn't get comfortable, so I gave him several °kicks that made him °grunt and stretch. He made room all right, though. Mother waked and felt for me. I settled back comfortably in the warmth of the bed with my °thumb in my mouth.

'Mummy!' I °hummed, loudly and contentedly.

'Sssh! dear,' she whispered. 'Don't wake Daddy!'

This was a new °development, which °threatened to be even more serious than 'talking to Daddy'. Life without my early-morning conferences was unthinkable.

'Why?' I asked severely.

'Because poor Daddy is tired.'

This seemed to me a quite °inadequate reason, and I was °sickened by the sentimentality of her 'poor Daddy'. I never liked that sort of °gush; it always struck me as insincere.

'Oh!' I said lightly. Then in my most winning tone: 'Do you know where I want to go with you today, Mummy?'

'No, dear,' she sighed.

'I want to go down the Glen and fish for °thornybacks with my new net, and then I want to go out to the Fox and Hounds, and—'

'Don't-wake-Daddy!' she °hissed angrily, clapping her hand across my mouth.

But it was too late. He was awake, or nearly so. He grunted and reached for

bolt upright ['bəult 'ʌp'rait] *kerzengerade*
rack one's brains [ræk, breinz] *sich den Kopf zerbrechen*
kick [kik] *(Fuß)Tritt*
grunt [grʌnt] *grunzen*

thumb [θʌm] *Daumen*
hum [hʌm] *summen, brummen*

development [di'veləpmənt] *Entwicklung*
threaten ['θretn] *drohen*

inadequate [in'ædikwit] *unangemessen*
sickened ['siknd] *angewidert*
gush [gʌʃ] *Gefühlserguß*

thorn(y)back ['θɔ:n(i)bæk] *Nagelrochen; Meerspinne*
hiss [his] *zischen*

the matches. Then he stared incredulously at his watch.

'Like a cup of tea, dear?' asked Mother in a meek, °hushed voice I had never heard her use before. It sounded almost as though she were afraid.

'Tea?' he exclaimed °indignantly. 'Do you know what the time is?'

'And after that I want to go up the Rathcooney Road,' I said loudly, afraid I'd forget something in all those interruptions.

'Go to sleep at once, Larry!' she said sharply.

I began to °snivel. I couldn't concentrate, the way that pair went on, and °smothering my early-morning schemes was like burying a family from the °cradle.

Father said nothing, but lit his pipe and °sucked it, looking out into the shadows without minding Mother or me. I knew he was °mad. Every time I made a remark Mother hushed me irritably. I was °mortified. I felt it wasn't fair; there was even something °sinister in it. Every time I had pointed out to her the waste of making two beds when we could both sleep in one, she had told me it was healthier like that, and now here was this man, this stranger, sleeping with her without the least °regard for her health!

He got up early and made tea, but though he brought Mother a cup he brought none for me.

'Mummy,' I shouted, 'I want a cup of tea, too.'

'Yes, dear,' she said patiently. 'You can drink from Mummy's saucer.'

°That settled it. Either Father or I

hushed [hʌʃt] *verhalten, gedämpft*
indignantly [in'dignəntli] *unwillig*

snivel ['snivl] *wimmern, schluchzen*
smother ['smʌðə] *unterdrükken*
cradle ['kreidl] *Wiege*

suck [sʌk] *saugen (an)*
mad [mæd] *verrückt, hier: wütend*
mortified ['mɔːtifaid] *gedemütigt, gekränkt*
sinister ['sinistə] *unheimlich, unheilvoll*

regard [ri'gɑːd] *Rücksicht*

that settled it ['setld] *damit war der Fall erledigt*

would have to leave the house. I didn't want to drink from Mother's saucer; I wanted to be treated as an equal in my own home, so, just °to spite her, I drank it all and left none for her. She took that quietly, too.

to spite her [spait] *um ihr „eins auszuwischen"*

But that night when she was putting me to bed she said gently:

'Larry, I want you to promise me something.'

'What is it?' I asked.

'Not to come in and disturb poor Daddy in the morning. Promise?'

'Poor Daddy' again! I was becoming °suspicious of °everything involving that quite impossible man.

suspicious [səs'piʃəs] *verdächtig*
everything involving that man [in'vɔlviŋ] *alles, was mit diesem Mann zusammenhing*

'Why?' I asked.

'Because poor Daddy is worried and tired and he doesn't sleep well.'

'Why doesn't he, Mummy?'

'Well, you know, don't you, that while he was at the war Mummy got the pennies from the Post Office?'

'From Miss MacCarthy?'

'That's right. But now, you see, Miss MacCarthy hasn't any more pennies, so Daddy must go out and find us some. You know what would happen if he couldn't?'

'No,' I said, 'tell us.'

'Well, I think we might have to go out and beg for them like the poor old woman on Fridays. We wouldn't like that, would we?'

'No,' I agreed. 'We wouldn't.'

'So you'll promise not to come in and wake him?'

'Promise.'

°Mind you, I meant that. I knew pennies were a serious matter, and I was all against having to go out and beg like

mind you [maind] *wohlgemerkt*

the old woman on Fridays. Mother laid out all my toys in a complete ring round the bed so that, whatever way I got out, I was bound to fall over one of them.

When I woke I remembered my promise all right. I got up and sat on the floor and played—for hours, it seemed to me. Then I got my chair and looked out the attic window for more hours. I wished it was time for Father to wake; I wished someone would make me a cup of tea. I didn't feel in the least like the sun; instead, I was bored and so very, very cold! I simply longed for the warmth and °depth of the big featherbed.

At last °I could stand it no longer. I went into the next room. As there was still no room at Mother's side I climbed over her and she woke with a start.

'Larry,' she whispered, °gripping my arm very °tightly, 'what did you promise?'

'But I did, Mummy,' I °wailed, caught in the very act. 'I was quiet for ever so long.'

'Oh, dear, and you're °perished!' she said sadly, feeling me all over. 'Now, if I let you stay will you promise not to talk?'

'But I want to talk, Mummy,' I wailed.

'That has nothing to do with it,' she said with a firmness that was new to me. 'Daddy wants to sleep. Now, do you understand that?'

I understood it only too well. I wanted to talk, he wanted to sleep—whose house was it, anyway?

'Mummy,' I said with equal firmness, 'I think it would be healthier for Daddy to sleep in his own bed.'

depth [depθ] *Tiefe*
I could stand it no longer *ich konnte es nicht länger aushalten*

grip [grip] *ergreifen, packen*
tightly ['taitli] *eng, fest*

wail [weil] *winseln*

perished ['periʃt] *umgekommen, hier: erfroren*

That seemed to °stagger her, because she said nothing for a while.

'Now, once for all,' she went on, °'you're to be perfectly quiet or go back to your own bed. Which is it to be?'

The injustice of it got me down. I had °convicted her out of her own mouth of °inconsistency and °unreasonableness, and she hadn't even attempted to reply. Full of spite, I gave Father a kick, which she didn't notice but which made him grunt and open his eyes in °alarm.

'What time is it?' he asked in a °panic-stricken voice, not looking at Mother but at the door, as if he saw someone there.

'It's early yet,' she replied °soothingly. 'It's only the child. Go to sleep again. ... Now, Larry,' she added, getting out of bed, 'you've wakened Daddy and you must go back.'

This time, °for all her quiet air, I knew she meant it, and knew that my principal rights and privileges were as good as lost unless I °asserted them at once. As she lifted me, I gave a °screech, enough to wake the dead, not to mind Father. He °groaned.

'That °damn child! Doesn't he ever sleep?'

'It's only a habit, dear,' she said quietly, though I could see she was °vexed.

'Well, it's time he got out of it,' shouted Father, beginning to °heave in the bed. He suddenly gathered all the bedclothes about him, turned to the wall, and then looked back over his shoulder with nothing showing only two small, °spiteful, dark eyes. The man looked very °wicked.

stagger ['stægə] *verblüffen, umwerfen*

you are to be *du hast zu sein, du mußt sein*
convicted [kən'viktid] *überführt*
inconsistency [inkən'sistənsi] *Unbeständigkeit, Wankelmut*
unreasonableness [ʌn'ri:znəblnis] *Unvernunft*

alarm [ə'lɑ:m] *Besorgnis, Unruhe*
panic-stricken ['pænikstrikən] *schreckerfüllt*

soothingly ['su:ðiŋli] *beruhigend*

for all her quiet air ['kwaiət 'ɛə] *trotz ihres ruhigen Auftretens*

assert [ə'sə:t] *behaupten*
screech [skri:tʃ] *Gekreisch*
groan [grəun] *stöhnen*
damn [dæm] = damned *verdammt*

vexed [vekst] *verärgert*
heave [hi:v] *sich (schwerfällig) erheben*

spiteful ['spaitful] *boshaft, gehässig*
wicked ['wikid] *böse*

To open the bedroom door, Mother had to let me down, and I broke free and dashed for the farthest corner, screeching. Father sat bolt upright in bed.

'Shut up, you little °puppy!' he said °in a choking voice.

I was so astonished that I stopped screeching. Never, never had anyone spoken to me in that tone before. I looked at him incredulously and saw his face °convulsed °with rage. It was only then that I fully realized how God had °codded me, listening to my prayers for the safe return of this °monster.

'Shut up, you!' I °bawled, °beside myself.

'What's that you said?' shouted Father, making a wild °leap out of the bed.

'Mick, Mick!' cried Mother. 'Don't you see the child isn't °used to you?'

'I see he's better fed than taught,' °snarled Father, waving his arms wildly. °'He wants his bottom smacked.'

All his previous shouting was as nothing to these °obscene words °referring to my person. They really made my blood boil.

'Smack your own!' I screamed hysterically. 'Smack your own! Shut up! Shut up!'

At this he lost his patience and °let fly at me. He did it with the lack of °conviction you'd expect of a man under Mother's °horrified eyes, and it ended up as a mere °tap, but °the sheer indignity of being °struck at all by a stranger, a total stranger who had °cajoled his way back from the war into our big bed as a result of my innocent °intercession,

puppy ['pʌpi] *junger Hund*
in a choking voice ['tʃəukiŋ, vɔis] *mit erstickter Stimme*

convulsed [kən'vʌlst] *krampfhaft verzerrt*
with rage [reidʒ] *vor Zorn*
cod [kɔd] *dial. foppen*
monster ['mɔnstə] *Ungeheuer*
bawl [bɔːl] *brüllen, kreischen*
beside myself [bi'said] *außer mir*
leap [liːp] *Sprung*

used to [juːst] *gewöhnt an*
snarl [snɑːl] *knurren*
he wants his bottom smacked [smækt] *er braucht ein paar hinten drauf*
obscene [əb'siːn] *ordinär*
referring to [ri'fəːriŋ] *sich beziehend auf*

he let fly at me [flai] *er stürzte sich auf mich*
conviction [kən'vikʃən] *Überzeugung(skraft)*
horrified ['hɔrifaid] *entsetzt*
tap [tæp] *Klaps*
the sheer indignity ['ʃiə in'digniti] *hier: die Erniedrigung allein*
struck [strʌk] *von* strike *schlagen*
cajole [kə'dʒəul] *schmeicheln*
intercession [intə'seʃən] *Vermittlung*

made me completely °dotty. I °shrieked and shrieked, and danced in my bare feet, and Father, looking awkward and hairy in nothing but a short grey army shirt, °glared down at me like a mountain out for murder. I think it must have been then that I realized he was jealous too. And there stood Mother in her nightdress, looking as if her heart was broken between us. I hoped she felt as she looked. It seemed to me that she deserved it all.

From that morning out my life was a hell. Father and I were enemies, open and °avowed. We conducted a series of °skirmishes against one another, he trying to steal my time with Mother and I his. When she was sitting on my bed, telling me a story, he took to looking for some pair of old boots which he °alleged he had left behind him at the beginning of the war. While he talked to Mother I played loudly with my toys to show my total lack of concern. He created a terrible scene one evening when he came in from work and found me at his box, playing with his regimental badges, Gurkha knives, and button-sticks. Mother got up and took the box from me.

'You mustn't play with Daddy's toys unless he lets you, Larry,' she said severely. 'Daddy doesn't play with yours.'

For some reason Father looked at her as if she had struck him and then turned away with a scowl.

'Those are not toys,' he growled, taking down the box again to see had I °lifted anything. 'Some of those °curios are very rare and valuable.'

dotty F ['dɔti] *verrückt*
shriek [ʃriːk] *schreien*
glare [glɛə] *starren*

avowed [ə'vaud] *erklärt*
skirmish ['skəːmiʃ] *Scharmützel*

allege [ə'ledʒ] *behaupten*

lift [lift] *stehlen*
curio ['kjuəriəu] *Kuriosität*

But as time went on I saw more and more how he managed to °alienate Mother and me. What made it worse was that I couldn't °grasp his method or see what attraction he had for Mother. In every possible way he was less winning than I. He had a common accent and made noises at his tea. I thought for a while that it might be the newspapers she was interested in, so I made up bits of news of my own to read to her. Then I thought it might be the smoking, which I personally thought attractive, and took his pipes and went round the house °dribbling into them till he caught me. I even made noises at my tea, but Mother only told me I was disgusting. It all seemed to °hinge round that unhealthy habit of sleeping together, so °I made a point of dropping into their bedroom and °nosing round, talking to myself, so that they wouldn't know I was watching them, but they were never up to anything that I could see. In the end it beat me. It seemed to depend on being grown-up and giving people rings, and I realized I'd have to wait.

But at the same time I wanted him to see that I was only waiting, not giving up the fight. One evening when he was being particularly °obnoxious, chattering away well above my head, °I let him have it.

'Mummy,' I said, 'do you know what I'm going to do when I grow up?'

'No, dear,' she replied. 'What?'

'I'm going to marry you,' I said quietly.

Father gave a great °guffaw out of him, but °he didn't take me in. I knew

alienate ['eiljəneit] *entfremden*
grasp [grɑːsp] *erfassen, begreifen*

dribble ['dribl] *sabbern, geifern*

hinge [hindʒ] *sich drehen um*
I made a point of [pɔint] *ich machte es mir zum Prinzip*
nose round ['nəuz 'raund] *herumspionieren*

obnoxious [əb'nɔkʃəs] *abscheulich*
I let him have it *ich gab es ihm*

guffaw [gʌ'fɔː] *schallendes Gelächter*
he didn't take me in *er konnte mich nicht hinters Licht führen*

it must only be °pretence. And Mother, in spite of everything, was pleased. I felt she was probably °relieved to know that one day Father's hold on her would be broken.

'Won't that be nice?' she said with a smile.

'It'll be very nice,' I said confidently. 'Because we're going to have lots and lots of babies.'

'That's right, dear,' she said °placidly. 'I think we'll have one soon, and then you'll have plenty of company.'

I was no end pleased about that because it showed that in spite of the way she gave in to Father she still considered my wishes. Besides, it would put the Geneys in their place.

It didn't turn out like that, though. To begin with, she was very °preoccupied—I supposed about where she would get the seventeen and six—and though Father °took to staying out late in the evenings it did me no particular good. She stopped taking me for walks, became as °touchy °as blazes, and smacked me for nothing at all. Sometimes I wished I'd never mentioned the °confounded baby—I seemed to have a genius for bringing calamity on myself.

And calamity it was! Sonny arrived in the most °appalling °hullabaloo—even that much he couldn't do without a fuss—and from the first moment I disliked him. He was a difficult child—so far as I was concerned he was always difficult—and °demanded far too much attention. Mother was simply silly about him, and couldn't see when he was only °showing off. As company he was worse than useless. He slept all day, and I had

pretence [pri'tens] *Vortäuschung*
relieved [ri'li:vd] *erleichtert*

placidly ['plæsidli] *beschaulich*

preoccupied [pri'ɔkjupaid] *in Anspruch genommen, beschäftigt*
he took to staying *er gewöhnte sich an zu bleiben*
touchy ['tʌtʃi] *empfindlich*
as blazes F ['bleiziz] *wie verrückt*

confounded [kən'faundid] *hier: verdammt*

appalling [ə'pɔ:liŋ] *entsetzlich*
hullabaloo ['hʌləbəlu:] *Spektakel*

demand [di'mɑ:nd] *fordern*
show off [ʃəu 'ɔf] *sich in Szene setzen*

to go round the house on tiptoe to avoid waking him. It wasn't any longer a question of not waking Father. The °slogan now was 'Don't-wake-Sonny!' I couldn't understand why the child wouldn't sleep at the proper time, so whenever Mother's back was turned I woke him. Sometimes to keep him awake I °pinched him as well. Mother caught me at it one day and gave me a most °unmerciful °flaking.

One evening, when Father was coming in from work, I was playing trains in the front garden. °I let on not to notice him; instead, I pretended to be talking to myself, and said in a loud voice: 'If another bloody baby comes into this house, I'm going out.'

Father stopped dead and looked at me over his shoulder.

'What's that you said?' he asked sternly.

'I was only talking to myself,' I replied, trying to °conceal my panic. 'It's private.'

He turned and went in without a word. Mind you, I intended it as a solemn warning, but its effect was quite different. Father started being quite nice to me. I could understand that, of course. Mother was quite sickening about Sonny. Even at mealtimes she'd get up and °gawk at him in the cradle with an idiotic smile, and tell Father to do the same. He was always polite about it, but he looked so puzzled you could see he didn't know what she was talking about. He complained of the way Sonny cried at night, but she only got cross and said that Sonny never cried except when °there was something up

slogan ['sləugən] *Schlagwort*

pinch [pintʃ] *zwicken*

unmerciful [ʌn'mə:siful] *mitleidlos*

a flaking *sl.* ['fleikiŋ] *eine Tracht Prügel*

I let on F *ich tat als ob*

conceal [kən'si:l] *verbergen*

gawk at [gɔ:k] *dumm anglotzen*

there was something up with him *es war etwas los mit ihm*

with him—which was a °flaming lie, because Sonny never had anything up with him, and only cried for attention. It was really painful to see how simple-minded she was. Father wasn't attractive, but he had a fine intelligence. He saw through Sonny, and now he knew that I saw through him as well.

One night I woke with a start. There was someone beside me in the bed. For one wild moment I felt sure it must be Mother, having come to her senses and left Father for good, but then I heard Sonny in convulsions in the next room, and Mother saying: 'There! There! There!' and I knew it wasn't she. It was Father. He was lying beside me, wide awake, breathing hard and °apparently as mad as hell.

After a while it came to me what he was mad about. It was his turn now. After turning me out of the big bed, he had been turned out himself. Mother had no consideration now for anyone but °that poisonous pup, Sonny. I couldn't help feeling sorry for Father. I had been through it all myself, and even at that age I was °magnanimous. I began to stroke him down and say: 'There! There!' He °wasn't exactly responsive.

'Aren't you asleep either?' he snarled.

'Ah, come on and put your arm around us, can't you?' I said, and he did, in a sort of way. °Gingerly, I suppose, is how you'd describe it. He was very bony but better than nothing.

At Christmas he went out of his way to buy me a really nice model railway.

a flaming lie ['fleimiŋ] *hier: eine verdammte Lüge*

apparently [ə'pærəntli] *offenbar*

that poisonous pup ['pɔiznəs] *hier: dieser Giftzwerg*

magnanimous [mæg'næniməs] *großmütig*

be responsive [ri'spɔnsiv] *entgegenkommend sein*

gingerly ['dʒindʒəli] *zimperlich*

A °Salesman's °Romance

BY FRANK O'CONNOR

MY friend, Charlie Ford, was a °commercial traveller in the °office-equipment business, and one of the nicest commercials I have known. And, in spite of all the propaganda against them, you meet some very nice commercials. At their best, they are °artists in their own right; people who make something out of nothing.

Charlie had only one °drawback from my °point of view, which was that he could never °resist trying to sell me things, just for practice. And they did not have to be office chairs or any other sort of °commodity. That is the sign of the true salesman; it isn't the money alone that appeals to him; it is °salesmanship for its own sweet sake.

Charlie, for instance, was from °Connemara, and °wild horses wouldn't have °dragged him back to it, but I could not mention Connemara over a drink without Charlie's trying to sell it to me, and the tears would come in his eyes and °a catch would come in his voice, and the °Mother Machrees and the evening °rosaries would get so colourful that nothing but °blasphemy would put a stop to them. Then he would smile sadly at me, put a fat hand firmly on my shoulder, and tell me in a deep voice that he wished I did not talk like a °wrecker. I wasn't a real wrecker, of course, not at heart. Other people might think so but he knew that at heart

salesman ['seilzmən] *Verkäufer; Handelsreisende*
romance [rəu'mæns] *Romanze*
commercial traveller [kə'mə:ʃəl 'trævlə] *Handelsreisende*
office equipment ['ɔfis i'kwipmənt] *Büroausstattung*
artists in their own right ['ɑ:tists] *hier: auf ihre Weise richtige Künstler*

drawback ['drɔ:bæk] *Nachteil*
point of view ['pɔint ɔv 'vju:] *Standpunkt, Ansicht*
resist [ri'zist] *widerstehen*

commodity [kə'mɔditi] *Artikel, Gebrauchsgegenstand*
salesmanship ['seilzmənʃip] *die Kunst des Verkaufens*
Connemara [kɔni'mɑ:rə] *Bergland in Galway, Irland*
drag [dræg] *schleppen*
wild horses wouldn't have dragged him back to it [waild 'hɔ:siz, 'wudnt] *keine zehn Pferde hätten ihn dorthin zurückgebracht*
a catch would come in his voice [vɔis] *seine Stimme pflegte zu stocken*
Mother *Klostervorsteherinnen werden mit* Mother *tituliert*
rosary ['rəuzəri] *Rosenkranz*
blasphemy ['blæsfəmi] *Gotteslästerung*

wrecker ['rekə] *Zerstörer, hier: Spötter*

I loved all those beautiful things as much as he did, and °concealed it only out of °modesty. And I declare to my God, before I knew where I was, Charlie would be selling me a substitute self with a heart of gold that the manufacturers would replace within two years unless it gave perfect satisfaction. All the same Charlie liked me. I was a sort of laboratory for him, and whenever he succeeded in selling me anything like a new °movie or a funny story, °it set him up for a week.

Charlie was °engaged to a girl called Celia Halligan. Celia was handsome, she had a dirty tongue and an attitude of cynical but good-humoured °contempt for men, yet even she could not resist the coloured enlargement of herself that Charlie presented to her in a °gilt frame, and he had only to give her a sweet, sad smile to make her °skip °demurely back into it.

Now, one night the two of them were motoring back from a pub outside °Rathfarnham, °cruising gently down the mountainside, admiring the °toylike, °whitewashed cottages above them and the valley of the city far below with the °lamplit °prow of °Howth °thrusting out into Dublin Bay, when all at once as they turned a corner, there was a °jaunting car ahead of them, °going hoppity-bump with no lights on the wrong side of the road. Charlie was a first-rate driver and °boasted that he had been driving for fifteen years without an accident. He did not °rush his car into the °ditch or try to °pass out. Instead, he °put his °brakes on hard and ran the °bonnet of his car under the

conceal [kən'si:l] *verbergen*
modesty ['mɔdisti] *Bescheidenheit*

movie ['mu:vi] *Film*
it set him up *es brachte ihn in Schwung*
engaged [in'geidʒd] *verlobt*

contempt [kən'tempt] *Verachtung*
gilt [gilt] *vergoldet*
skip [skip] *springen*
demurely [di'mjuəli] *sittsam, gesetzt, zurückhaltend*
Rathfarnham [ræθ'fɑ:nəm] *Dorf 3 Meilen südlich von Dublin*
cruise [kru:z] *langsam dahinfahren*
toylike ['tɔilaik] *spielzeughaft, winzig*
whitewashed ['waitwɔʃt] *weiß getüncht*
lamplit ['læmplit] *von Lampen erhellt*
prow [prau] *Bug, Vorderteil (meist von Schiffen)*
Howth [həuθ] *Ort in der Grafschaft Dublin*
thrust [θrʌst] *stoßen, hier: hinausragen*
jaunting car ['djɔ:ntiŋ kɑ:] *leichter, zweirädriger Karren mit Längssitzen*
going hoppity-bump ['hɔpiti bʌmp] *dahinholpernd*
boast [bəust] *sich rühmen*
rush [rʌʃ] *stürzen*
ditch [ditʃ] *Graben*
pass out [pɑ:s 'aut] *ausscheren*
brake [breik] *Bremse*
put the brakes on hard *scharf bremsen*
bonnet ['bɔnit] *Kühlerhaube*

°well of the jaunting car without doing any more °damage than to raise the driver and °pitch him gently forward on the back of his old horse. The bump was so slight that the °jarvey's °bowler hat still remained on his head, and the horse, who had all the sense of °responsibility °required by the situation, stopped dead with the jarvey °plastered affectionately across his back, and waited for somebody to do something.

Then presence of mind came to the jarvey's assistance: he judged the road and the steadiness of the horse and the intentions of the driver behind him, and °slid gently to the ground. It was as neat a bit of work as Charlie had seen in years. By the time Charlie reached him, °he was doing a convincing take-off of unconsciousness that °deceived even Celia.

'Is that fellow dead, Cha?' she asked anxiously.

'No, dear, only °stunned,' Charlie replied °comfortingly, but it was he who felt stunned. He knew he had a ripe and subtle intelligence to deal with. Then he cursed softly because he heard two °cyclists talking as they pushed their bikes up the hill. The jarvey heard them too, and lay °doggo till all the proper questions had been asked. Then he opened his °red-rimmed eyes and asked °feebly:

'Where am I?'

'In the presence of °witnesses,' °retorted Charlie who couldn't resist it. The jarvey, a small man with a thin, °mournful face that had the blue °glaze of the confirmed alcoholic all over it, looked at him °reproachfully. Charlie

well [wel] *Laderaum*
damage ['dæmidʒ] *Schaden*
pitch [pitʃ] *werfen, schleudern*
jarvey ['dʒɑːvi] *(Mietsdroschken) Kutscher*
bowler hat ['bəulə hæt] *Melone (Hut)*
responsibility [rispɔnsə'biliti] *Verantwortung*
require [ri'kwaiə] *verlangen*
plastered ['plɑːstəd] *angeklebt*

slid [slid] *von* slide *rutschen*
he was doing a convincing take-off of unconsciousness [ʌn'kɔnʃəsnis] *er spielte überzeugend einen Ohnmachtsanfall vor*
deceive [di'siːv] *täuschen*

stun [stʌn] *betäuben*
comfortingly ['kʌmfətiŋli] *tröstend*

cyclist ['saiklist] *Radfahrer*
doggo *sl.* ['dɔgəu] *regungslos*
red-rimmed ['redrimd] *rotumrändert*
feebly ['fiːbli] *schwach*

witness ['witnis] *Zeuge*
retort [ri'tɔːt] *erwidern*
mournful ['mɔːnful] *traurig*
glaze [gleiz] *Glanz, Glasigkeit*
reproachfully [ri'prəutʃfuli] *vorwurfsvoll*

could smell the whisky off him from the side of the road.

When they had found a farm-labourer to look after the horse and car the jarvey, whose name turned out to be Clarke, °permitted himself to be driven to hospital, and an °over-conscientious medical student decided to °detain him for the night, while Charlie went off to report the accident to °the guards with a certain sour satisfaction at the thought of the presence of mind that enabled a °boozy little man like that to seize on a moment's opportunity and turn it into a career.

permitted himself to be driven ['drivn] *ließ sich fahren*
over-conscientious ['əuvəkɔnʃi'enʃəs] *(all)zu gewissenhaft*
detain [di'tein] *behalten, zurückhalten*
the guards *Pl* [gɑ:dz] *die Wache*
boozy ['bu:zi] *beschwipst*

And a career it looked like becoming. The °solicitor for the insurance company, an old friend of Charlie's called Cronin, agreed to defend the case, but this was °mainly on Charlie's account because Charlie felt about his driving as good women feel about their reputation. You could call Charlie a °sex-fiend and he only smiled; you could call him a swindler and he positively °chortled, but suggest that he hadn't taken proper °precautions at a corner and you were in danger of losing a friend.

solicitor [sə'lisitə] *Anwalt*
mainly ['meinli] *hauptsächlich*

sex-fiend ['seksfi:nd] *Sexteufel, -besessener*
chortle ['tʃɔ:tl] *frohlocken*
precaution [pri'kɔ:ʃən] *Vorsichtsmaßnahme*

As the weeks went by, the jarvey's case grew like a masterpiece in the mind of a great artist. It looked as if it would never stop. After months he was still in bed, because, according to himself, he got °reelings when he rose.

reelings ['ri:liŋz] *Schwindelanfälle*

'Ah, it's the girl,' said Cronin, a cheerful, noisy little man who was never depressed about anything except the law.

'What has Celia to do with it?' Charlie asked sternly.

'You'll soon see when they ask you what you were doing with her in the car,' said Cronin °gloomily. 'I told you to let the case go.'

'But that's scandalous,' Charlie said hotly. 'I'm not the man to do °that sort of thing when I'm driving.'

'You're not like hell,' said Cronin cynically, leaving Charlie uncertain whether to take it as a compliment or not.

Altogether it was a shocking experience for Charlie. He was a man of °eager temperament, not the sort to have a thing like that hanging over him for months, and he had the illusion, common to eager men, that all he had to do to °speed it up was to °call regularly on Cronin whose office was in a little lane off Dame Street, a sunless °hole where Charlie could not imagine any °prosperous professional man °choosing to work. Usually he had to wait for half an hour in the outer office with secretaries as unattractive as the room, and passed the time in trying to sell them his version of the °accident. When °finally he was °admitted and learned that nothing had happened, he burst into a long °tirade to which Cronin listened, sitting back in his chair balancing a pencil and looking °bored and depressed. Charlie could not stop trying to sell you things, and again he tried to sell Cronin the scandalous story of the drunken jarvey, and the idea that he should bring a °counter-suit against the jarvey, but he was beginning to see that you couldn't sell a lawyer a °safety-pin even if his °braces had °burst.

gloomily ['glu:mili] *düster*
that sort of thing *so etwas*
eager ['i:gə] *lebhaft*
speed up [spi:d 'ʌp] *beschleunigen*
call on ['kɔ:l ɔn] *besuchen*
hole [həul] *Loch*
prosperous ['prɔspərəs] *erfolgreich, wohlhabend*
choose [tʃu:z] *wählen*
accident ['æksidənt] *Unfall*
finally ['fainəli] *endlich*
admit [əd'mit] *zugeben, zulassen; ein-, vorlassen*
tirade [tai'reid] *Wortschwall*
bored [bɔ:d] *gelangweilt*
counter-suit ['kauntəsju:t] *Gegenklage*
safety-pin ['seiftipin] *Sicherheitsnadel*
braces ['breisiz] *Hosenträger*
burst [bə:st] *bersten, platzen*

'You don't understand these things, Charlie,' Cronin said °wearily, leaning farther back in his chair and playing patiently with his pencil. 'Linnane isn't going to do anything like that. This is a °jury case, and juries are °trickier than judges and judges are trickier than the devil. You're a fine-looking, well-dressed man, and by your own account this jarvey is a °shrimp. Now, what happens if you get a jury of shrimps is that they'll decide the poor shrimp in the box °is entitled to °compensation for life from the insurance company. °They can damn well afford it. If you were a shrimp you'd feel the same. Forget about the °booze!'

By the time °the case came up for hearing, Charlie was feeling a °wreck. For two nights he hadn't slept, going carefully over all the points on which the other side might try to °trap him, and all the sins of his past life that they might °resurrect against him. °Counsel for the jarvey was an old °acquaintance of Celia's called Michael Dunn, and Charlie hoped that on this account he might show some consideration. On the other hand, if he decided not to do so, he would know more about Charlie than was desirable. It was a bad business. He went to °court with Celia, feeling like death, and saying in a dull voice that he didn't know if he'd ever be able to drive again. It would hang over him for the rest of his days, and it was °blackmail, and everyone knew it was blackmail, but the State permitted it and the lawyers °encouraged it. Celia said nothing at all. She thought it would have been cheaper to buy off the

wearily ['wiərili] *müde*
jury case ['dʒuərikeis] *Geschworenengerichtsverhandlung*
tricky ['triki] *riskant, heikel*

shrimp [ʃrimp] *Knirps, Wicht*
be entitled to [in'taitld] *Anspruch haben auf*
compensation [kɔmpen'seiʃən] *Wiedergutmachung*
they can afford it [ə'fɔ:d] *sie können es sich leisten*
booze F [bu:z] *Alkohol (als Getränk)*

the case came up for hearing ['hiəriŋ] *der Fall kam zur Verhandlung*
wreck [rek] *Wrack, nur noch ein Schatten seiner selbst*
trap [træp] *eine Falle stellen*
resurrect [rezə'rekt] *auferstehen, hier: wiederaufleben lassen*
counsel ['kaunsəl] *Rechtsbeistand, (Rechts)Anwalt*
acquaintance [ə'kweintəns] *Bekannte*

court [kɔ:t] *Hof; Gerichtshof*

blackmail ['blækmeil] *Erpressung*
encourage [in'kʌridʒ] *ermutigen*

jarvey for a few pounds. She was going to a dance that night with another man. She had asked Charlie to bring her but he had refused. He even thought it heartless of her, considering that he was a man with no future. And there, at the other end of the seat from him was the jarvey who had °blasted his career, looking sick and resigned, his bowler hat on the seat beside him.

Charlie °leant forward over the seat ahead of him as he concentrated on the first case, and his depression grew because he didn't understand a word of it. The judge was an oldish man with pink cheeks and white hair. He seemed to be °deaf and °irritated by everybody. Then the jarvey's case was called and Michael Dunn °rose. He was a tall, °ascetic-looking man with a neat black °moustache and big, dark glasses. To his °alarm, Charlie noticed that no considerations of friendship seemed to °restrain him in the °remarks he made.

The jarvey himself was called and went slowly up the court-room, looking as though he might drop dead at any moment. He answered questions in an °ailing voice that was °barely audible from the °jury-box. He had the jarvey's °technique of °plausibility, and treated the court as if it were a party of American tourists he was taking on a °conducted tour of the Lakes of °Killarney. He pointed to the places where he felt the pains as though they were of historic importance. As for reward, he indicated that he was an unworldly little man with no notion of the value of money, and he left it entirely to the natural °generosity of his °fares. Charlie began

blast [blɑːst] *zerstören, vereiteln, vernichten*
leant [lent] *von* lean *sich lehnen*

deaf [def] *taub*
irritated ['iriteitid] *gereizt*
rose [rəuz] *von* rise *sich erheben*
ascetic [ə'setik] *asketisch, enthaltsam*
moustache [məs'tɑːʃ] *Schnurrbart*
alarm [ə'lɑːm] *Bestürzung, Besorgnis*
restrain [ri'strein] *zurückhalten*
remark [ri'mɑːk] *Bemerkung*

ailing ['eiliŋ] *kränklich, leidend*
barely audible ['bɛəli 'ɔːdibl] *kaum hörbar*
jury-box ['dʒuəribɔks] *Geschworenenbank*
technique [tek'niːk] *Technik, Methode*
plausibility [plɔːzə'biliti] *Glaubwürdigkeit, Wahrscheinlichkeit*
conducted tour [kən'dʌktid 'tuə] *Besichtigungsfahrt, Führung*
Killarney [ki'lɑːni] *Stadt in Kerry, Irland*
generosity [dʒenə'rɔsiti] *Großmut*
fare [fɛə] *Fahrgast*

to realize that Cronin and Linnane had known what they were about. He knew the technique and °despised it. It was the technique of the poor mouth.

Fortunately, it became °obvious after a quarter of an hour that the judge thought he was trying another case and was °confusing the jarvey with a °truck driver who had been hit by a railway wagon. Michael Dunn in his attempt at getting his Lordship on to the right track went into °convulsions of °deference, almost suggesting that there wasn't really much difference between a jaunting car and a truck, but the judge wasn't having any. He had been °insulted and he was going to °take it out on somebody. He got down behind his bench as though he were taking up a firing position from which to °decimate the court.

'I'd be very pleased if Counsel would realize that °I still have my wits about me,' he snapped.

'I beg your Lordship's pardon,' said Dunn. 'I wasn't suggesting for an instant—'

'And though I may not be quite as young as Counsel, I still know the difference between a truck and a jaunting car,' said the judge, and he continued to make comments which ignored witness and counsel till the poor jarvey's pose was completely broken down and he was °yelling. The atmosphere of the conducted tour had been completely °dissipated.

That did the trick. Charlie had been growing more and more °disgusted, more and more terrified, as his own turn drew nearer. Then as he strolled

despise [dis'paiz] *verachten*

obvious ['ɔbviəs] *offenbar*
confuse with [kən'fju:z wið] *verwechseln mit*
truck driver ['trʌk 'draivə] *Lastwagenfahrer*

convulsion [kən'vʌlʃən] *Krampf, Zuckung*
deference ['defərəns] *Ehrerbietung*
insult [in'sʌlt] *beleidigen*
take it out on somebody *seine Wut an j-m auslassen*

decimate ['desimeit] *dezimieren, stark schwächen*
I have my wits about me [wits] *ich bin bei Verstand*

yell [jel] *gellend schreien*
dissipate ['disipeit] *zerstreuen, in nichts auflösen*

disgusted [dis'gʌstid] *angeekelt*

slowly up the court-room to the witness stand he had a sudden moment of °revelation and joy. He recited the °oath in a °thrilling voice that made it perfectly clear that here at least was a man who knew the meaning of words. The judge glanced at him with the air of a child who sees a new toy. Charlie bowed very low to the judge, who was so astonished that he bowed back, then he bowed—not quite so low—to the jury, gave them a winning smile, and sat down, crossing his legs. In that moment of revelation he had seen that the °wretched °occupants of the court °were distracted with °boredom, and he knew that the only cure for boredom was to buy something. The whole country was mad with boredom because it had been °brought up to count every penny. To express your °faith in life it was necessary to buy a °stake in the future.

So Charlie °proceeded to sell the jury the story which no °lawyer would buy. He took Linnane's questions for what they should have been rather than what they were, and °disposed of them as though they were no more than the °promptings of a good listener. He demonstrated exactly how the supposed accident had occurred, using his hands, his feet, and his magnificent voice till even the judge turned into a possible customer. He threw in amusing little °side-swipes at the °County Council and the condition of the roads, at the habits of Irish motorists, and—completely ignoring Cronin's warning—at the jarvey's drunkenness as well. Dunn was on his feet at once, protesting, but the

revelation [revi'leiʃən] *Erleuchtung*
oath [əuθ] *Eid*
thrilling ['θriliŋ] *mitreißend, packend*

wretched ['retʃid] *elend, unglücklich*
occupants ['ɔkjupənts] *hier: Anwesende*
boredom ['bɔːdəm] *Langeweile*
be distracted with boredom [dis'træktid] *hier: sich tödlich langweilen*
brought up [brɔːt 'up] *von* bring up *erziehen*
faith [feiθ] *Glaube*
stake [steik] *Spieleinsatz, Anteil*
proceed [prə'siːd] *fortfahren*
lawyer ['lɔːjə] *Rechtsanwalt*

dispose of [dis'pəuz əv] *verfügen über, behandeln*
promptings ['prɔmptiŋz] *hier: Stichworte*

side-swipe ['saidswaip] *Seitenhieb*
County Council ['kaunti 'kaunsl] *Grafschaftsrat, Verwaltungsbehörde einer Gr.*

judge had still not forgiven him his unmannerly correction and °snubbed him. He said that Charlie struck him as an honest and observant witness who told his story in a °straightforward and, above all, °audible way.

Even when Dunn got up to cross-examine, Charlie did not feel in the least °rattled. On the contrary. He no longer saw Dunn as an inquisitor with °subtle °devices for forcing him to °reveal the secrets of his past life, but as a wrecker, a man without °confidence, the sort of small-town expert who °sneers at even the finest office furniture. Charlie put on the air of melancholy °suitable to such a °mean-spirited wretch. Dunn, who had a trick of looking away as though °in search of inspiration, tried to suggest to Charlie that he was speaking from °depths of meditation that no one had ever reached.

'Mr Ford,' he said, looking at Charlie °contemptuously over the big horn-rimmed spectacles, 'you °ventured to °suggest that my client was under the influence of liquor on the night in question. Now, before we go any further, perhaps you wouldn't mind °enlightening the court as to where you and your lady friend were coming from?'

'Not in the least,' Charlie replied sweetly. 'We were coming from the Red Cow.'

'The Red Cow?' repeated Dunn, who was under the illusion that to look at the ceiling and repeat a name as though he had never heard it before was a good way of making it seem °significant. 'Would I be correct in °assuming that the Red Cow is a °hostelry?'

snub [snʌb] *zurechtweisen, rügen*
straightforward ['streit'fɔː-wəd] *geradeheraus*
audible ['ɔːdəbl] *hörbar*

rattled F ['rætld] *verwirrt*
subtle ['sʌtl] *fein, schwer deutbar, fast unmerklich*
device [di'vais] *Mittel, Handhabe*
reveal [ri'viːl] *enthüllen, verraten*
confidence ['kɔnfidəns] *Vertrauen*
sneer at [sniə] *spotten über*
suitable ['sjuːtəbl] *passend*
mean-spirited ['miːnspiritid] *gemein, niedrig denkend*
in search of [səːtʃ] *auf der Suche nach*
depth [depθ] *Tiefe*

contemptuously [kən'temp-tjuəsli] *verächtlich*
venture ['ventʃə] *wagen*
suggest [sə'dʒest] *vorschlagen, andeuten*
enlighten [in'laitn] *aufklären*

significant [sig'nifikənt] *bedeutsam*
assume [ə'sjuːm] *annehmen*
hostelry ['hɔstəlri] *Gaststätte (veraltet od. poetisch)*

'You'd hardly be correct in assuming it, Mr Dunn,' Charlie replied with quiet amusement. °'Assumptions are made about things of which we have no direct knowledge.'

There was a °chuckle from the jury-box at this, and Dunn grew red and went on in a hurry.

'And did you have some—um—refreshment there?'

'Yes, sir,' Charlie said °meekly. 'That is generally my °purpose in going to a °bar.'

Dunn pointed at the judge.

'Tell my lord and the jury how many drinks you had.'

'Three,' Charlie said °steadily. 'You see, Mr Dunn, it was a very hot night, and I'd been driving for a good part of the day, so I was rather thirsty.'

'And you ask the court to believe that after three drinks—on a very hot night—when you'd been driving for a good part of the day, as you've admitted—you were still °capable of driving a car °properly?'

'I ask the court to believe that if I wasn't capable of driving properly I wouldn't be driving at all,' said Charlie °sternly.

'The guards made no test to °ascertain if you were capable of driving?'

'I °presume the guards °are aware that there is no test known to science that will °prove the existence of lemonade in the °system,' replied Charlie.

Of course, Charlie didn't know whether there was or not, nor was there much danger of his being examined about it if there was. For several of the jurymen laughed °outright and even the

assumption [ə'sʌmpʃən] *Annahme*
chuckle ['tʃʌkl] *leises Lachen*

meekly ['mi:kli] *sanft, bescheiden, demütig*
purpose ['pə:pəs] *Zweck*
bar [bɑ:] *Bar, Schanktisch, Büfett*

steadily ['stedili] *fest, unerschüttert*

capable ['keipəbl] *fähig*
properly ['prɔpəli] *ordentlich*

sternly ['stə:nli] *ernst, streng*
ascertain [æsə'tein] *sich vergewissern*
presume [pri'zju:m] *annehmen*
be aware [ə'wɛə] *sich bewußt sein*
prove [pru:v] *beweisen*
system ['sistim] *Organismus*

outright [aut'rait] *unverhohlen*

judge gave a smile of °glee. His own style of wit was rather like that.

'You mean you drink nothing but lemonade?' asked Dunn, who was beginning to °lose his temper and with good °reason, for it was not often that he had a witness like Charlie to °deal with. But Charlie was beginning to get tired of him; he knew that if he was to complete his sale he must °crush this knowing customer, so he paused a moment before replying.

'I mean nothing of the sort, Mr Dunn,' he said °gravely. 'I mean that a man who drinks anything stronger when he's °in charge of a car is a dangerous °lunatic.'

'An exceedingly proper remark,' said the judge, nodding four times and knocking his bench in °approval. Nothing goes down so well in a court of law as a °well-aimed °platitude.

Dunn had given up hope of °shaking this °unruly man, and °contented himself with a few °perfunctory questions °intended to suggest that Charlie and Celia had been too busy in the car to pay attention to the road.

'This young lady and you are friends?' asked Dunn.

'No, Mr Dunn,' Charlie said gently. 'Just engaged.'

'And you hadn't your arm about her shoulder?'

'Ah, no, Mr Dunn,' Charlie said wearily. 'You and I ought to be beyond the °adolescent stage.'

This produced a real roar and after a few further °efforts Dunn sat down and °pretended to be °absorbed in his papers. Charlie bowed again to the judge

glee [gli:] *Heiterkeit*

lose one's temper [lu:z, 'tempə] *die Geduld verlieren*
reason ['ri:zn] *Grund, Ursache*
deal with [di:l] *zu tun haben mit*
crush [krʌʃ] *niederschmettern, vernichten*

gravely ['greivli] *ernst*
in charge of [tʃɑ:dʒ] *verantwortlich für*
lunatic ['lu:nətik] *Narr*
approval [ə'pru:vəl] *Anerkennung*
well-aimed ['weleimd] *wohlgezielt*
platitude ['plætitju:d] *Gemeinplatz, Banalität*
shake [ʃeik] *hier: erschüttern*
unruly [ʌn'ru:li] *unlenkbar, widerspenstig*
he contented himself [kən'tentid] *er gab sich zufrieden*
perfunctory [pə'fʌŋktəri] *oberflächlich, flüchtig*
intend [in'tend] *beabsichtigen*

adolescent stage [ædəu'lesnt steidʒ] *Jünglingsalter*
effort ['efət] *(angestrengter) Versuch, Bemühung*
pretend [pri'tend] *vorgeben*
absorbed in [əb'sɔ:bd] *vertieft in*

and jury and returned to his seat with the °transfigured °air of a man who has been to the altar. Cronin °winked at him, but Charlie °failed to return the wink. Instead he smiled °wanly, and closing his eyes, covered them with his fat hand. Charlie of course knew as well as Cronin did that the case was in the bag. Charlie, the universal salesman, had sold his story to the jury and °nothing short of an earthquake would °break the spell he had woven about them.

But then it was Celia's turn, and Charlie's heart sank when he saw that she had learned nothing from his example. Instead of taking the oath as though she had been waiting months for it, °she had it extracted from her word by word like teeth. She looked beautiful and angry, and what was worse, alarmed, and Charlie knew within a few moments that her unhappiness was °spreading to the court-room. She replied to Linnane's friendly questions as though he were cross-examining her, and when Dunn rose she gave him a positive °scowl. Charlie hoped that as an old friend of the family he might show some sense of °decency, but °he was still smarting under Charlie's thrusts.

'And were you also drinking lemonade, Miss Halligan?' he asked with his shoulders °hunched while he °jingled the coins in his trousers pockets.

'Ah, I was not,' she snapped with a °shrug. °'I wouldn't touch the blooming stuff.'

Charlie had noticed the impressive effect of a platitude; now he noticed the effect of a simple °statement of °preju-

transfigured [træns'figəd] *verklärt*
air [ɛə] *Miene*
wink at [wiŋk] *zublinzeln*
he failed to return the wink [feild] *er reagierte nicht auf das Blinzeln*
wanly ['wɔnli] *schwach, matt*

nothing short of an earthquake ['ə:θkweik] *nur ein Erdbeben*
break the spell [breik, spel] *den Zauber brechen*

she had it extracted from her [iks'træktid] *sie ließ ihn (den Eid) sich herausziehen*
spread [spred] *(sich) ausbreiten*

scowl [skaul] *finsterer Blick*
decency ['di:snsi] *Anstand*
he was still smarting under Charlie's thrusts ['smɑ:tiŋ] *er hatte Charlies Angriffe noch nicht verwunden*

hunched [hʌntʃt] *gekrümmt*
jingle ['dʒiŋgl] *klimpern*
shrug [ʃrʌg] *Achselzucken*
I wouldn't touch the blooming stuff *so einen Mist rühre ich nicht an*
statement ['steitmənt] *Feststellung*
prejudice ['predʒudis] *Vorurteil*

dice. A °shudder seemed to go through the court.

'Tell the court what you were drinking.'

'I was drinking whisky, of course,' she replied in a shrill, shocked tone. 'What do you think?'

Dunn bent forward and looked at her satanically over his glasses.

'I have no opinion, Miss Halligan,' he said °reprovingly. 'I merely wish to find out if at the time of this accident you weren't a little—°elevated, shall we say?'

'Is it after three small ones?' she asked °incredulously. 'What do you take me for?'

At this point Linnane tried to go to Celia's °rescue, but the judge had taken an instant dislike to her. The judge lived in hope that one of these days he would find one of those modern girls before him so that he could say what he really thought about them. He knew it would make °headlines, and like most judges he longed for headlines. He had a strong suspicion that Celia was a modern young woman. He told her that this was a court of law, and he would not permit her to reply to counsel in that °impudent fashion, °at which Celia, who had no intention of being impudent, looked °mutinous as well as angry. He held the case up for several minutes to °glower at her, waiting for a back-answer that would give the opportunity he wanted. Dunn knew that the signals were set at clear for him, and though Linnane again intervened, the judge °snorted that the witness appeared to be

shudder ['ʃʌdə] *Schauder*

reprovingly [ri'pru:viŋli] *tadelnd*
elevated ['eliveitid] *erhöht, hier: angeheitert*
incredulously [in'kredjuləsli] *ungläubig*

rescue ['reskju:] *Rettung*

headline ['hedlain] *Überschrift, Schlagzeile*

impudent ['impjudənt] *frech, unverschämt*
at which *worauf*
mutinous ['mju:tinəs] *aufrührerisch, rebellisch*
glower ['glauə] *finster od. grollend blicken*

snort [snɔ:t] *schnauben*

one of those modern young women, so she probably expected to be dealt with in a modern way.

Charlie covered his face entirely. °To give him his due, he went through agonies. As Dunn °framed each question, he answered it in his own mind, °tossing off the awkward ones with light feminine °banter, °lingering gravely over those that °raised moral issues; smiling, frowning, and even prepared to shed a tear behind his hands. And on top of the ideal reply came the real one, all in one tone, °bewildered and maddened and sounding as though it came from the lips of some international °courtesan. Dunn made her admit that she was often at the Red Cow, that she had gone there for years with different men; that she had been kissing Charlie in the car before they started, and almost trapped her into saying that she was in no state to describe what had happened. 'Salesmanship!' Charlie thought despairingly. 'That's what °the girl lacks. Salesmanship!'

She came down off the stand, °sulky and furious. Charlie rose and stepped out into the °passageway with an °angelic, welcoming smile to let her into the seat beside him, and tried to put his hand comfortingly on hers, but she pushed past him °as though he were to blame for everything and °stalked out of the court. He had to wait for the °verdict, and though it represented victory for him, it brought him no satisfaction. It even left him wondering why he had gone to all that trouble instead of allowing the insurance company to buy off the jarvey.

to give him his due [djuː] *um ihm Gerechtigkeit zu erweisen*
frame a question [freim] *eine Frage formulieren*
tossing off the awkward ones ['ɔːkwəd] *indem er über die peinlichen rasch hinwegging*
banter ['bæntə] *Neckerei, Scherz*
lingering ['liŋgəriŋ] *verweilend*
raise an issue [reiz, 'iʃuː] *ein Problem aufwerfen*
bewildered [bi'wildəd] *verwirrt*
courtesan [kɔːti'zæn] *Kurtisane, Dirne*
the girl lacks [læks] *dem Mädchen fehlt*
sulky ['sʌlki] *mürrisch, trotzig*
passageway ['pæsidʒwei] *Korridor, Durchgang*
angelic [æn'dʒelik] *engelhaft*
as though [ðəu] *als ob*
stalk [stɔːk] *stolzieren*
verdict ['vəːdikt] *Urteil*

Next morning in town he ran into a °gossipy woman who had heard all about the case and wanted to talk of it.

'And I saw Celia at the dance last night,' she went on °joyously. 'And I'll give you three guesses who she was dancing with.'

'Who, Babe?' asked Charlie, °kidding her on.

'Michael Dunn!'

'Dunn?' Charlie asked incredulously. 'Are you sure, Babe?'

'Sure, I saw her, I tell you. He went up and talked to her, and they were laughing and joking, and the next thing was I saw them dancing. Now, what do you make of that?'

'I don't know what to make of it, Babe,' Charlie said, shaking his head gravely. 'I'd hardly have expected it of her.'

But Celia gave him no satisfaction at all. She seemed surprised and irritated by his °attitude.

'But why wouldn't I dance with him?' she asked. 'Sure, he only did what he was paid for, the same as anyone else. He'd do the same thing to his own mother. Did you ever know a lawyer that wouldn't?'

But °reasonable as she made it sound, it carried no °conviction to Charlie. Reason had never yet made a woman friendly to a man she had cause to dislike. Could it be that she hadn't really resented Dunn's tone? That she might even have enjoyed it?

He was still more °upset when she returned the ring and told him she was marrying Dunn. Charlie was a °rational man, and like all rational men took the

gossipy ['gɔsipi] *klatschsüchtig*
joyously ['dʒɔiəsli] *freudig, fröhlich*
kidding her on ['kidiŋ] *indem er sie durch Neckerei zum Weiterreden anregte*
attitude ['ætitju:d] *Haltung, Einstellung*
reasonable ['ri:znəbl] *vernünftig*
conviction [kən'vikʃən] *Überzeugung*
upset [ʌp'set] *aufgeregt, aufgebracht*
rational ['ræʃənl] *vernünftig*

irrational hard. It wasn't only the loss of Celia that hurt him, though that was bad enough; it wasn't even the unfairness of her going to the Red Cow with Dunn, as he saw her do with his own eyes. It was the unreasonableness of it all. °He took to the drink, and for months it looked as if he would never be himself again. °Woebegone and °haggard, he went over every detail of it with his friends a hundred times. But gradually as he repeated it, he began to realize that it was an excellent story, a story you could sell to °prospective customers. 'Did I ever tell you,' he would ask with a °wistful smile, 'how I won the case and lost the girl?'

Suddenly, Charlie was himself again. Art had triumphed over Nature. It was the old story—'Out of my great °sorrows I made little songs.'

he took to the drink *er begann zu trinken*
woebegone ['wəubigɔn] *verhärmt*
haggard ['hægəd] *abgezehrt, hager*
prospective customer [prə'spektiv 'kʌstəmə] *potentieller Kunde*
wistful ['wistful] *wehmütig*
sorrow ['sɔrəu] *Sorge, Leid*

As Joe Said . . .

By Herbert Sutherland

'Now don't forget,' my mother said, 'that the °view from °Durham station is the finest view in the world. And what else have you got to do?'

'Write home every week,' I said.

'And what have you *not* got to do?'

'Play cards.'

'Yes. And remember, if you meet Willy, you have to salute him the same as everybody else, even if he is your brother. It's the °rule.'

The trouble with mother was, she wouldn't realize I'd grown up.

A porter was coming along the platform °slamming doors. There were two fellows sitting in the carriage behind me.

'They'll be for the infantry,' my mother said, noticing my look. 'The °Royal Corps of Signals take only the best. You have to have a °School Cert. at least.'

The porter was getting nearer. I turned to go into the carriage.

'That man with the long nose,' my mother whispered, 'I don't like him.' She had another look at him. 'Still, he'll be going into the infantry.'

The way mother spoke you felt he was already dead.

The train started, and it wasn't till we were out of the station that I remembered I hadn't waved.

The fellow with the long nose spoke.

'Signals?'

'Yes.'

view [vjuː] *Aussicht*
Durham ['dʌrəm] *Stadt in der Grafschaft Durham, Nordengland*

rule [ruːl] *Reglement, Vorschrift*

slam [slæm] *zuschlagen (Türe)*

Royal Corps of Signals ['rɔiəl, kɔː, 'signəlz] *Königliche Nachrichtentruppe*
School Cert. [sə'tifikit] *Abkzg für* certificate *Zeugnis; hier: Zeugnis einer höheren Schule*

°'Darlington?'

'Yes.'

'We're Signals too. I'm Joe Fisher, this is Andy Bates.'

Andy was tall like Joe, only fair.

I °introduced myself a bit °self-consciously. You're always a bit self-conscious when your Christian name's Herbert and it's the only one you've got.

'We were just wondering,' Joe said, 'if you'd °fancy a little game of °brag?'

'Oh, sure,' I said.

I °missed the view from Durham station, I had a pair of queens. I missed the view from °Ferryhill too, but maybe that was all right. I didn't °recollect my mother saying anything about Ferryhill.

We nearly went on after Darlington, but they had a fellow going round, a °sergeant or something, telling people to °get off. So Joe put the cards in his pocket just as they were, and we °assembled on the °platform like a lot of °sheep waiting to be °dipped, then tramped in a long °straggly line through the snow to the °drill hall. Somebody started to sing.

The three of us landed up in the same company together, and once we'd got our beds made, we continued the game, and the two months we were in Darlington that game never stopped. Of course there were times when we didn't play—when we were asleep for instance, or when we °were on guard. By stopping, I mean, the cards were never °shuffled. In brag, you just °stick them on the bottom at the end of a round and keep dealing from the top.

Darlington ['dɑːliŋtən] *Stadt in der Grafschaft Durham*

introduce oneself [intrə'djuːs] *sich vorstellen*

self-consciously ['self'kɔnʃəsli] *befangen*

fancy ['fænsi] *hier: Lust haben auf*

brag [bræg] *Name eines Kartenspiels*

miss [mis] *vermissen, versäumen*

Ferryhill ['ferihil] *Marktflecken südlich von Durham*

recollect [rekə'lekt] *sich erinnern*

sergeant ['sɑːdʒənt] *Feldwebel*

get off [get 'ɔf] *aussteigen*

assemble [ə'sembl] *sich versammeln*

platform ['plætfɔːm] *Bahnsteig*

dip [dip] *eintauchen*

sheep waiting to be dipped *Sch., die auf das Eintauchen warten (Sch. werden durch ein Bad mit einem Insektenbekämpfungsmittel getrieben)*

straggly ['strægli] *(weit) auseinandergezogen, unordentlich*

drill hall ['dril'hɔːl] *Exerziersaal*

be on guard [gɑːd] *Wache schieben*

shuffle ['ʃʌfl] *(Karten) mischen*

stick on [stik 'ɔn] *ankleben, hier: drunterschieben*

Actually, that game lasted from January 17th, 1940, till the °Japs °packed in in 1945.

Most of the time in Darlington we spent in the football ground with flags in our hands sending °messages to each other. As Joe said, it made you °realize how °browned off a windmill must get.

Then from Darlington we moved to °Liverpool. That was °when °Dunkirk was on. I was never so happy to leave a place in all my life. Joe had got hold of some °field cards, and I must have crossed the wrong line out because my mother turned up with my aunt Ethel and °raised cain with the °colonel. We were having a quiet little game at the time, and the colonel wanted to know what I meant by writing home saying I was wounded and in hospital. And mother said it was a °disgrace our °idling our time when France had fallen and would the colonel please °post Joe?

We °got stuck on °bayonet practice after that, running up and down shouting, and ramming the blade through some sacks filled with straw. As Joe said, it was all very well, but what was the other °bloke doing when you were sticking a bayonet in him?

We played °solid on the boat, except for the ten days we got separated after °Cape Town.

It was a bit of bad luck that. Actually, we weren't going ashore at all, but a bloke I'd known from the university happened to be on the ship, and °tagged on, and I thought I'd better have a look round just in case he wrote to my mother. The old lady was a great one on culture and broadening the mind.

Japs [dʒæps] *Abkzg für* Japanese
pack in [pæk 'in] *einpacken, hier: den Krieg aufgeben*
message ['mesidʒ] *Nachricht*
realize ['riəlaiz] *sich bewußt werden od. vergegenwärtigen*
browned off *sl.* [braund 'ɔf] *gelangweilt*
you realize ... must get *man kann sich vorstellen, wie fade einer Windmühle zumute ist (Der signalgebende Soldat wird wegen seiner Stellungen mit einer Windmühle verglichen.)*
Liverpool ['livəpu:l] *Hafenstadt in Westengland*
Dunkirk [dʌn'kə:k] *französische Hafenstadt a.d. Nordsee*
when Dunkirk was on *als Dünkirchen aktuell war (Im 2. Weltkrieg schnitten die Deutschen 1940 bei D. die brit.-franz. Nordarmee ab.)*
field card ['fi:ld kɑ:d] *Feldpostkarte*
raise cain [reiz kein] *Krach schlagen*
colonel ['kə:nl] *Oberst*
disgrace [dis'greis] *Schande*
idle one's time ['aidl] *seine Zeit vertrödeln*
post [pəust] *wegschicken, hier: auf den Kriegsschauplatz schicken*
got stuck on [gɔt, stʌk] *von* get..., *hier: nichts tun als*
bayonet ['beiənit] *Bajonett, Seitengewehr*
bloke [bləuk] *Kerl*
solid ['sɔlid] *ohne Unterbrechung*
Cape Town ['keiptaun] *Kapstadt (Hafenstadt i.d. Südafrikanischen Union)*
tag on [tæg] *sich anhängen*

Well—we managed to °dodge this bloke in a pub by the old fort, at least I think it was the old fort, it had thick walls anyway, and were on the way back to the ship, when a bloke called Scotty stopped in a big car and just wouldn't take no.

dodge [dɔdʒ] *ausweichen, hier: sich verdrücken vor*

We got in, and were taken to this hotel. There were a whole lot of girls there, blondes, brunettes, all good lookers. °We were °due back at the ship at ten, but Scotty said no, he'd fixed it with our colonel, and we had to stay the night, he'd °laid on a big party for us. A dark fellow showed us to our rooms. There was a small card table in Joe's. We had a wash and shave, then Joe suggested a quick hand before we went downstairs for °sundowners or whatever they called them.

due [dju:] *fällig*
we were due at ten *wir mußten um 10 Uhr zurück sein*
laid on [leid'ɔn] *von* lay on *planen, vorbereiten*

sundowner ['sʌndaunə] *Dämmerschoppen*

That was one of the best games I can ever remember. Andy's watch had stopped, and it wasn't till this Zulu brought breakfast in, that we realized we'd been playing all night. We played solidly all the next day, then at ten o'clock, when it was dark, Scotty came in and said he was sorry but he'd have to take us back to the ship as the °convoy was sailing at two o'clock that morning. He wouldn't have time to see the colonel, but he had a letter already typed that would fix everything.

convoy ['kɔnvɔi] *Geleitzug*

We came out of the ship's prison just before °Colombo. We didn't °bother to °go ashore there, nor at Bombay where we were °stuck for a week. At Port Tewfik, in Egypt, it was different. We had to get off. That was our °destination.

Colombo [kə'lʌmbəu] *Hauptstadt von Ceylon*
bother ['bɔðə] *sich die Mühe machen od. nehmen*
go ashore [ə'ʃɔ:] *an Land gehen*
stuck [stʌk] *von* stick *festsitzen, hängenbleiben*
destination [desti'neiʃən] *Bestimmungsort, Ziel*

They °mucked us around so much in Cairo—we got stuck in different tents, and twice in one week this °press gang came along and took us to the pyramids—that when an Australian battalion asked for three cooks, we °volunteered. Actually, it was a big °decision °on my part, for I'd just got a letter from my mother two months old asking me if my °commission had come through yet.

muck around *sl.* [mʌk ə'raund] *herumschleifen*
press gang ['pres gæŋ] *eine in früheren Jahrhunderten verwendete Gruppe von Soldaten, welche junge Männer mit Gewalt zum Militärdienst zwangen*
volunteer [vɔlən'tiə] *sich freiwillig melden*
decision [di'siʒən] *Entscheidung*
on my part [pɑːt] *meinerseits*
commission [kə'miʃən] *Offizierspatent, Ernennung zum Offizier*

It was a good move that, and as regards cooking, as Joe said, you couldn't °harm the °grub much if you just left it in the tin and warmed it up. We got in some good games then—we were °static at the time—but the °advance spoiled it a bit. And actually, even that wasn't too bad. Our worst moment was when Joe's shirt got blown off his back with °blast at °Sidi Barrani. We thought the game was finished then, but we found the shirt in a petrol tin about a hundred yards away. It was in °shreds, but the cards were O.K. The breast pocket hadn't been touched. As Joe said, it was probably a good thing, as it °brought home to you the horrors of modern war.

harm [hɑːm] *schaden*
grub *sl.* [grʌb] *Futter, Fraß*
static ['stætik] *bewegungslos, hier: nicht im Einsatz*
advance [əd'vɑːns] *Vormarsch*
blast [blɑːst] *Explosion, Luftdruck, Sprengladung*
Sidi Barrani ['sidi bə'rɑːni] *Hafenstadt in Ägypten*
shred [ʃred] *Lappen, Fetzen*
brought home to s.o. [brɔːt] *von* bring… *j-m klarmachen*

At °Benghazi, or some place like that, °we got sent back to °Alexandria, and I went into hospital with a °boil on my leg, but Andy and Joe used to come up every day and we had many a quiet game in the night sister's °shower. Then one day, it was a Sunday, Joe came running into the °ward. I'd never seen Joe run before, and for one awful moment I thought he'd lost the cards.

°'You got to get out, Herb,' he said,

Benghazi [ben'gɑːzi] *Hafenstadt in Libyen*
we got sent back *sl.* = we were sent back
Alexandria [ælig'zɑːndriə] *Hafenstadt in Ägypten*
boil [bɔil] *Furunkel*
shower ['ʃauə] = shower-bath *Brausebad*
ward [wɔːd] *Krankenstation*
you got to get out *sl.* = you have got to get out *du mußt heraus*

'we're sailing this afternoon for England!'

It was like trying to get out of a graveyard when you're dead.

We saw everybody, from the bloke °in charge—he was a °brigadier or a general or something—to the °dhobi °wallah—but no, no °discharges on a Sunday. As Joe said, they didn't seem to realize there was a war on. In the end, I climbed the wall—Joe had a taxi laid on—and we °made the ship with half an hour to spare.

be in charge [tʃɑːdʒ] *Verantwortung haben, diensthabend*
brigadier [brigə'diə] *Brigadekommandeur*
dhobi ['dəubi] *indisch Wäscher*
wallah ['wɔlə] *indisch Mann*
discharge [dis'tʃɑːdʒ] *Entlassung*
make *hier: erreichen*

We ran into a storm the next day, and lost the convoy, but after five days of wandering round, Gibraltar was sighted. It didn't look much like Gibraltar, not the way Cape Town did with °Table Mountain and that, and we were just settling down for a °hand when a sergeant with a red face told us to get off.

Table Mountain ['teibl 'mauntin] *Tafelberg (in Kapstadt)*
hand *Karten in der Hand eines Spielers, das Blatt; auch ein Kartenspiel; eine Runde*

I tried a °spot of Spanish on some of the °locals, but they didn't seem to understand.

a spot [spɔt] *hier: ein Stückchen, ein wenig*
the locals ['ləukəlz] *die Einheimischen*

We travelled a bit in a °truck. It was a tricky job trying to lay the cards flat on account of the °bumping, and we'd just °got the hang of it, when the truck stopped, and they put us in a tent. We'd just started a fresh hand when my brother Willy turned up, he was a major now, and said it would be our last chance to see the °Acropolis before the °Jerries started. I said I thought the Acropolis was in Greece, and Willy said where the hell did we think we were, Spain? As Joe said, the army tells you nothing.

truck [trʌk] *Lastauto*
bumping ['bʌmpiŋ] *Poltern, Stoßen*
got the hang of s.th. [gɔt, hæŋ] *von* get ... *hinter etwas kommen, den „Dreh 'rauskriegen"*
Acropolis [ə'krɔpəlis] *hochgelegene Burg von Athen*
Jerries ['dʒeriz] *Spitzname für die Deutschen*

Well, we went round, and Willy said he'd see us the next day and we'd do the

Acropolis properly—he had a degree in history—but fortunately the war must have started again, and we got sent north. After about four days we stopped in some mountains, put a tent up, and dug in.

It was the next day, when we were having a quiet little hand, that Joe said there seemed to be an awful lot of °planes about. Somebody blew a whistle just then, and Joe said we'd better go and have a look in case it was a gas °drill. The officers used to get °real mad if they found you playing without a °respirator on.

The sky was full of falling °parachutes, you could see the men °waggling their legs as they dropped. 'Into the °trenches!' somebody shouted. We °piled into one. There was firing going on all over. It was death to raise your head. Then somebody further along the trench started shouting that all the °rifles were back in the tents.

The section officer, a little bloke called Watson, called for volunteers to get the arms and show the Jerries what was what.

Joe started to write a letter home, the first since he'd left England. Andy Bates was showing a bloke I didn't know a few tricks with a piece of string, and me?—well, I put two new °laces in my boots.

Somebody said, 'Hey Joe, your tent's on fire!'

Joe put his letter down and looked over the trench.

It was the bravest thing I ever saw, and what did Joe get for it—nothing! There were °shells and °bullets °whizzing all

plane [plein] *Kurzform für* aeroplane
drill [dril] *Exerzieren, hier: Probeangriff*
real *sl.* ['riəl] = really
respirator ['respəreitə] *Gasmaske*
parachute ['pærəʃu:t] *Fallschirm*
waggle ['wægl] *baumeln mit*
trench [trentʃ] *Schützengraben*
pile [pail] *sich drängen*
rifle ['raifl] *Flinte*
laces ['leisiz] = shoe-laces *Schuhbänder*
shell [ʃel] Granate
bullet ['bulit] *Gewehrkugel*
whizz [wiz] *sausen, zischen*

over, and old Joe, he just climbed over that trench and walked across slow to the tent °like he was going to school.

'Brave man!' somebody shouted.

How he lived, we never knew, for he'd just got to the tent when it burst into flames. He came out after a bit, taking his time back, and °patting out the small fires on his clothes.

°'Where's the °flaming rifles?' Lt. Watson suddenly screamed.

'Rifles?' Joe said. 'What rifles?'

He dropped into the trench and handed the cards to Andy. °It was Andy's deal. The battle was °raging outside, but Lt. Watson, he seemed to °go berserk. He got Joe by the collar and started shaking him and shouting at him, that in the end, we moved to another trench. As Joe said, you can't deal properly if somebody's trying to °choke you.

We got out of Greece by taking a °dhow that didn't seem to belong to anybody and pointing its nose south. A number of German °aircraft flew low over us once or twice to see who we were, and an Italian °submarine °trailed us for a bit, but on the whole they left us alone. The Allies were the worst. Twice a °R.N. °corvette °hove to and told us to °put in at °Crete. And the third time the bloke got really nasty saying that not only would he confiscate the cards but he would shoot Joe personally as well. But as Joe said, when Crete was °a day astern, he didn't like the look of Crete, there seemed to be an awful lot of bombing going on there, and anyway, how were we to

like he was going *sl.* = as if he were going

pat out [pæt] *ausklopfen, ausschlagen*

where's *sl.* [wɛəz] = where are

flaming ['fleimiŋ] *hier: verdammt*

it was Andy's deal [di:l] *Andy war mit Geben dran*

rage [reidʒ] *wüten*

go berserk [bə:'sə:k] *wild werden*

choke [tʃəuk] *erwürgen, ersticken*

dhow [dau] *Dau (arab. Segelschiff)*

aircraft ['ɛəkrɑ:ft] *Flugzeug(e)*

submarine ['sʌbmə'ri:n] *Unterseeboot*

trail [treil] *hier: verfolgen*

R.N. *Abkzg für* Royal Navy *Königl. Marine*

corvette [kɔ:'vet] *Korvette, kleines Kriegsschiff*

hove to [həuv] *von* heave to *stoppen, beidrehen*

put in at *(Seemannssprache: einen Hafen) anlaufen*

Crete [kri:t] *Kreta (griech. Insel)*

a day astern [ə'stə:n] *eine Tages(see)reise hinter uns*

know it *was* Crete, there was no notice board up like you see in railway stations.

We got to Alexandria all right, then they sent us to Jerusalem. I don't remember much about Jerusalem, except that Joe got °a running flush queen high there against Andy Bates's pair of kings, and the bloke in the next bed said he'd just seen °Nelson Eddy in the *New Moon* or something and we shouldn't miss it.

a running flush queen high [flʌʃ] *eine geschlossene Kartenreihe („Flöte") bis hinauf zur Königin*
Nelson Eddy ['nelsən 'edi] *ein Filmschauspieler*

We joined an Australian battalion in °Nazareth, and we got a bit of peace, except when Joe lent his rifle to a °Digger who sold it to an Arab for ten dinar, and we had an awful job getting it back. °The Aussies were easy about it, but the British got really nasty. Still, as Joe said, it was *their* rifle and the market price was fifteen dinar.

Nazareth ['næzəriθ] *Stadt in Israel*
Digger ['digə] *Spitzname für einen austral. Soldaten*
the Aussies ['ɔziz] *Spitzname für die Australier*

After fighting °the Vichy French for a bit, or maybe it was the Turks—people seemed to keep changing sides so much—we got sent to °Baghdad. We got in some good games there, then we moved north to stop the Russians, or was it the Germans? Anyway, whoever it was they didn't come, and then we got sent to °Burma.

the Vichy French ['vi:ʃi:] *die Franzosen, die im 2. Weltkrieg mit den Deutschen kollaborierten. Sitz der Regierung war in V., Mittelfrankreich*
Baghdad ['bægdæd] *Hauptstadt des Irak*
Burma ['bə:mə] *Staat in Hinterindien*

It was tough there. Sometimes, during the °monsoon, the cards got so °damp they would stick, and you had to be careful you didn't deal two together. And then, when 2 Div. °relieved us, it got dry, and we had an awful job keeping the °ants away from those cards. A fellow Joe knew, a Scotsman, lost a whole pack one night in two hours, they just ate the lot.

monsoon [mɔn'su:n] *Monsun*
damp [dæmp] *feucht*
relieve [ri'li:v] *ablösen, erlösen*
ant [ænt] *Ameise*

Oh, we °went through it!

went through it [went] *von go... etwas durchmachen od. erleben*

°Then if Willy didn't turn up. He was a full colonel now, and I was taken off cookhouse, and our colonel °had me teaching Latin to some °rookies just out from home. We were resting at the time. I still kept the same tent though, but it used to get pretty °grim at night with blokes wandering in and stopping the game to decline °*mensa* or °show off with a few irregular verbs. Joe got really mad one night, and said that a bloke either liked playing cards or he didn't, and I'd have to make my mind up. And I didn't dare tell Joe, Willy had just got at our colonel and they were going to send me to °O.C.T.U. Sometimes I could hardly concentrate on the game °for worry.

Then our colonel got killed. I don't know whether it was °suicide or typhus. Maybe it was the enemy. I was at the funeral anyway, then the order came that men who had three years eight months in °abroad had to be sent home.

We had five years in then, but they sent us home just the same, and we landed up in Düsseldorf, Germany, when the Jerries had packed in.

It wasn't bad in Düsseldorf, with Willy still out in Burma, only they used to °turf us off to the Asta Nielsen cinema twice a week, and lock the door so you couldn't get out. However, we °got in with the °projectionist, a nice fellow called Karl or Otto or something —he'd lost a leg in °Stalingrad—and he used to let us play in the operating room.

Then one day, in the °billets—it was a nice room, you could see the Rhine or the Weser or whatever it was called

Then if Willy didn't turn up *Dann tauchte zu allem Überfluß auch noch Willy auf*
had me teaching *ließ mich unterrichten*
rookie *sl.* ['ruki] *Rekrut, Anfänger*
grim [grim] *grimmig, gereizt*
mensa *lat. Tisch*
show off *prahlen*
O.C.T.U. *Abkzg für* Officer Cadets Training Unit
for worry ['wʌri] *vor lauter Sorge*
suicide ['sjuisaid] *Selbstmord*
abroad [ə'brɔːd] *im Ausland*
turf off *sl.* [təːf] *schicken, stekken*
got in with *sl.* [gɔt] *von* get ... *sich anfreunden mit*
projectionist [prə'dʒekʃənist] *Filmvorführer*
Stalingrad ['stɑːlingræd] *im 2. Weltkrieg schwer umkämpfte russ. Stadt an der Wolga*
billets ['bilits] *(Privat) Quartier*

just across the street, I never got time to ask—Joe was dealing. I'd just taken up my hand, when a little °fascist called Tommy Tulip ran into the room shouting, 'The Japs have packed in! The Japs have packed in!' and started kicking the walls.

'O.K.' Joe said, to °humour him, he was making such a noise, 'so they packed in. Who were they fighting?'

I don't know why, but Tommy seemed to think that was funny although Joe wasn't joking, he was just trying to get rid of him, and after °sniggering a bit, Tommy suddenly °grabbed the cards and flung them in the air, and went out °whooping.

It was the worst moment of the whole war.

Joe covered his face with his hands, and I remember my throat went so dry I could hardly swallow.

But worse was to come.

Andy bent down to pick up the cards. °He seemed to have aged in the last few minutes °had Andy. Then he did a thing no one had thought to do in the last five and a half years.

He counted the cards.

'Oh, my God,' he said, 'fifty-one!'

Joe was crying openly.

Outside, a man °coughed, and a ship hooted on the °Volga.

You could hear them °cheering all over the building. Some of the Germans were even cheering in the streets. They're like that, the Germans, they'll cheer anything.

'Fifty-one,' Andy repeated.

As Joe said, it made you feel the whole war had been in vain.

fascist ['fæʃist] *Faschist (hier als Schimpfwort gebraucht)*

humour s.o. ['hju:mə] *j-m willfahren, eingehen auf j-n*

snigger ['snigə] *kichern*

grab [græb] *schnell ergreifen, packen*

whoop [hu:p] *schreien, rufen, jubilieren*

He seemed ... had Andy *Andy schien tatsächlich ... gealtert zu sein*

cough [kɔf] *husten*

Volga ['vɔlgə] *Wolga*

cheer [tʃiə] *hurra rufen; (zu)-jubeln*

Langenscheidts Taschenwörterbuch Englisch

Teil I: Englisch-Deutsch
Von Helmut Willmann, 672 Seiten.

Teil II: Deutsch-Englisch
Von Heinz Messinger und Gisela Türck. 720 Seiten.

Beide Teile auch im Komplettband. Format jeweils 9,6 × 15,1 cm. Langenscheidts Taschenwörterbuch Englisch mit einem Wortschatz von rund 120 000 Stichwörtern und Wendungen in beiden Teilen. Für Schule, Beruf, Alltag und Reise sowie die fremdsprachliche Lektüre.

Langenscheidts Großes Schulwörterbuch Englisch

Teil I: Englisch-Deutsch
Von Heinz Messinger. 1380 Seiten.

Teil II: Deutsch-Englisch
Von Dr. Sonia Brough. 1384 Seiten.
Format jeweils 11,5 × 19 cm. Gebunden.

In beiden Teilen finden sich rund 220 000 Stichwörter und Wendungen. Ebenfalls in dieser Reihe erscheint „Lateinisch-Deutsch" (mit 30 000 Stichwörtern) sowie Französisch-Deutsch und Deutsch-Französisch mit rund 210 000 Stichwörtern und Wendungen.

Englisch fürs Gespräch

256 Seiten, Format 11 × 18 cm, kartoniert-laminiert.

Angefangen von der Begrüßung bis zu Themen wie Verkehr, Wirtschaft, Sport und Kunst werden hier idiomatische Redewendungen und Ausdrükke zur Verfügung gestellt, mit denen zusätzliche Sicherheit in der Unterhaltung mit dem fremdsprachigen Gesprächspartner gewonnen werden kann. Auch für Französisch, Italienisch, Spanisch.

1000 englische Redensarten

240 Seiten, illustriert, Format 12,4 × 19,2 cm, kartoniert-laminiert.

Eine Zusammenstellung idiomatischer Wendungen, die zum vollen Verständnis fremder Sprachen unentbehrlich sind. Der Inhalt der Bände ist nach Stichwörtern alphabetisch geordnet. Auch für Deutsch, Französisch, Italienisch, Spanisch.

Teste Dein Englisch!

Von Geoffrey Broughton.
Format 11 × 18 cm, kartoniert-laminiert.

In einem anregenden und amüsanten Frage- und Antwortspiel lernt der Benutzer, wie man die für den Ausländer typischen Fehler vermeidet. Die lustig illustrierten Textbücher werden von Schülern und Erwachsenen im Selbstunterricht, sowie im Unterricht benutzt.

Stufe 1: Testbuch für Anfänger. 208 Seiten.
Stufe 2: Testbuch für Fortgeschrittene. 222 Seiten.
Stufe 3: Testbuch für Könner. 224 Seiten.

ein weiterer Titel dieser Reihe:

Teste Dein Business English!

Von Susan Goldblatt.
120 Seiten, Format 11 × 18 cm, kartoniert-laminiert.